ANNETTE YATES
AND NORMA MILLER

THE SLOW COOKER SECRET

RIGHT WAY

Constable & Robinson Ltd
55-56 Russell Square
London WC1B 4HP

www.constablerobinson.com

First published in the UK 2006 under the title *Fresh Ideas For Your Slow Cooker*

Fully revised edition published by Right Way, an imprint of Constable & Robinson, 2009

This illustrated edition published by Right Way, an imprint of Constable & Robinson Ltd, 2011

A copy of the British Library Cataloguing in
Publication Data is available from the British Library

ISBN 978-0-71602-302-9

Printed and bound in China

10 9 8 7 6 5 4 3 2 1

Designed by: www.basementpress.com

Pictures Credits

www.shutterstock.com p.8 © Robyn Mackenzie, p.23 © Monkey Business Images, p.24 © Margoe Edwards, p.30 © Judy Kennamer, p.36 © grintan, p.40 © Teresa Kasprzycka, p.43 © Karin Hildebrand Lau, p.46 © Jiri Hera, p.51 © Juriah Mosin, p.52 © David P. Smith, p. 60 © margouillat photo, p.62 ©wasa_d, p.65 © Studio Foxy, p.66 © Roberto Zilli, p.68 © bonchan, p.72 © Shebeko, p.76 © IRA, p.79 © Hywit Dimyadi, p.80 © Gregory Gerber, p.82 © Robyn Mackenzie, p.84 © Cbenjasuwan, p.88 © zkruger, p.90 © Barbro Bergfeldt, p.93 © Baloncici, p.94 © Christy Liem, p.96 © Elena Schweitzer, p.98 © Bochkarev Photography, p.101 © Kirsanov, p.108 © AISPIX, p.112 © vsevolod izotov, p.116 © Joe Gough, p.118 © Jovan Nikolic, p.122 © Monkey Business Images, p.128 © Joe Gough, p.142 © shtukicrew, p.145 © nito, p.146 © Eugen Wais, p.148 © ravl, p.150 © Michael C. Gray, p.154 © IngridHS, p.165 © Kati Molin, p.166 © Fabio Alcini, p.168 © Cheryl Casey, p.172 © mates, p.174 © Stefan Fierros, p.176 © Eva Gruendemann, p.179 © dtlbg, p.180 © Lilyana Vynogradova, p.184 © kiboka, p.185 © erkanupan, p.186 © magnola, p.188 © Matt Hart

www.istockphoto.com p.18 © Charles Islander, p.35 © darren wise, p.48 © Paul Cowan, p.54 © Lauri Patterson, p.124 © Joe Gough, p.127 © Lauri Patterson, p.130 © whitewish, p.132 © Joe Gough, p.160 © Yula Zubritsky, p.162 © Grzegorz Malec

www.alamy.com p.74 © Bon Appetit, p.115 © Bon Appetit, p.136 © Martin Lee, p.153 © Bon Appetit

CONTENTS

INTRODUCTION

S LOW COOKING IS IN vogue. Tender and succulent joints of meat and the rich, subtle flavours of slow-cooked dishes are again in favour. An appetising prospect, certainly, but how can you achieve these results in your own kitchen? With busy modern lifestyles, most of us just cannot manage to have food roasting, braising or simmering all day long in the oven or on the hob. The solution to this conundrum is your slow cooker. This economical and versatile machine can be trusted to produce wonderful, traditional and innovative meals, ready just when you want them, while you go out and about doing other things.

Using fresh and store-cupboard ingredients, lots of exciting spices and aromatic herbs, our fully-tested and foolproof recipes are designed to obtain the maximum benefit from your slow cooker. Starting with our lazy breakfasts, there are ideas for dishes throughout the day and for every day: high days and holidays, weekdays and weekends alike. There are small-scale meals for one or two, and dishes for large parties, family or friends. Plenty of serving suggestions and hints and tips accompany the recipes.

You can travel the world with your slow cooker. After all, slow cooking is the time-honoured foundation to many of the finest global cuisines. You can create surprises too. Just look at our section on cakes. And you can slow-cook rice, pasta and grains as well. When you do have all day to prepare for a large gathering, and your oven and hob are fully utilised, your slow cooker can add significantly to your capacity for catering on a grand scale. And don't forget how energy saving your slow cooker is, when compared with the cost of producing equally sumptuous fare by conventional means.

By bringing slow cooking up to date and combining the traditional and contemporary, we can all have the dishes we most want to eat, dishes for where and who we are.

QUICK-CHECK RECIPE INDEX

1.

HINTS & TIPS

This section is all about how to get the best from your slow cooker and from our recipes.

- Just like most kitchen appliances, slow cookers are likely to vary from model to model. Always be guided by your manufacturer's instructions. In particular, check their recommendation for the minimum and maximum quantity of food, and preheating.

- You will need to get a feel of the cooking times too – when you first try out recipes in this book, compare the cooking times with similar ones in your manufacturer's instruction book. You may find you need to adjust our timings slightly to suit your slow cooker. If your slow cooker has only one setting (i.e. it cannot be switched to High, Medium or Low) you may need to shorten cooking times in this book by between 30 minutes and one hour.

- The cooking time on High is generally just under half that on Low. To shorten the cooking time of a recipe cooked on Low (perhaps on a day when you arrive home early and want to speed things up), switch the slow cooker to High setting and halve the remaining time.

- When adapting conventional recipes for the slow cooker, reduce the quantity of liquid by about half and use these cooking times as an approximate guide:

Conventional	In the Slow Cooker		
	Low	*High*	*Auto*
½ hour	6–8 hours	3–4 hours	5–7 hours
½–1 hour	8–10 hours	5–6 hours	6–8 hours
1–3 hours	10–12 hours	7–8 hours	8–10 hours

- To encourage even cooking of ingredients, cut them into even-size pieces.

- As meat cooks more quickly than vegetables, cut the vegetables into small dice or thin slices.

- Always thaw frozen foods before putting them in the slow cooker.

- Browning meat and vegetables on the hob before adding them to the slow cooker will usually give a better colour and flavour to soups, stews and casseroles.

- Dried beans and whole peas (and some whole lentils) often need an overnight soak in plenty of cold water before boiling rapidly for 10 minutes, draining and adding to the slow cooker.

Red kidney beans **must always** be boiled rapidly for 10 minutes. Always check the packet instructions.

- Rice? Easy-cook varieties usually produce the best results.

- Season only sparingly until the dish is cooked – flavours tend to concentrate in the slow cooker and you may find you need less salt, for example, than normal.

- Some quick-cooking ingredients are best added towards the end of cooking, such as rice, pasta and grains, and vegetables that you want to stay crisp or retain their bright colour. Others, like cream or milk, are likely to separate if added more than 30 minutes before the end of cooking.

- By all means lift the lid to check or stir occasionally. Each time you do, remember to add about 15 minutes to the cooking time to compensate for the loss of heat.

The Recipes

- For convenience, the ingredients are listed in the order in which they are used. Though they are given in imperial as well as metric, you will find the metric measurements easier to use.

- Most of the recipes can be doubled to make extra servings.

- Sometimes you may want to cook a small quantity of food in a large slow cooker. Simply follow the method in the recipe and transfer the prepared ingredients to an ovenproof dish that will fit comfortably inside the slow cooker. Cover the dish securely with foil and add boiling water to come half-way up its sides. Cover the slow cooker with the lid and cook as normal.

- The recipes include basic store-cupboard ingredients, including the occasional stock cube and, our favourite, vegetable bouillon powder. Because it's granular, you can spoon out as little as you like.

- All spoon measures are level unless otherwise stated.

- One or two recipes may contain partly cooked eggs – please remember that it is advisable to avoid eating these if you are pregnant, elderly, very young or sick.

- Sometimes we use a stick blender for whizzing soups into chunky or smooth blends (alternatively you could use a food processor).

- Some recipes contain fresh chillies. Do take care when preparing them and remember to wash your hands thoroughly afterwards. Better still, wear rubber gloves while handling them.

- We usually suggest preheating the slow cooker before using, but do check with your manufacturer's instructions to see if this is strictly necessary for your model.

2. LAZY BREAKFASTS

Is this your morning to relax and take it easy? After a busy working week or a late night entertaining, with guests staying over, breakfast needs to be there when you want it and hassle-free. Your slow cooker gives you this freedom and flexibility, and the food, when cooked, will stay hot.

About half of the recipes in this section can be left to cook overnight and will be ready when you are for breakfast. The rest can be started in the morning and are ideal for a late breakfast going on brunch. So there will be time for you, your family and your guests to read the newspapers, take the dog for a walk or even go to the gym.

For feeding large numbers, some of these recipes can easily be doubled in quantity.

Weekend Porridge

This porridge, with whole oats, lightly spiced, and with added fruit and seeds, is lovely on a cold winter morning. To make it plain, simply omit the spices, fruit and seeds.

SERVES 6–8

LOW 7–10 hours

175g/6 oz large rolled oats
1 tsp mixed spice
4 tbsp raisins
2 tbsp seeds, such as sunflower and pumpkin, plus
   extra for serving

Clear honey, soft brown sugar or demerara sugar,
   to serve
Milk or single cream, to serve

1   Preheat the slow cooker on High while you prepare the ingredients. Put the kettle on to boil.

2   Put the oats into the slow cooker and add the mixed spice, raisins and seeds. Pour over 1.3 litres/2¼ pints hot water (from the kettle) and stir well.

3   Cover with the lid and cook on Low for 7–10 hours, by which time the oats should be very tender and the porridge will have thickened. Stir well.

4   Ladle into bowls and drizzle with clear honey or sprinkle with brown or demerara sugar and a little milk or cream spooned over the top of each serving. Sprinkle with extra seeds if wished.

BREAKFAST FRUIT

We prefer to cook the fruit one day and chill it overnight, ready for spooning over hot porridge (see previous page) the next morning. If preferred, it can of course be eaten warm from the slow cooker. We like it for dessert too, with thick yogurt or vanilla ice cream.

SERVES 8

LOW 6–10 hours

500g/1 lb 2 oz mixed dried fruit, such as apples, apricots, figs, peaches and prunes
Small handful of raisins or sultanas
3 whole cloves or a good pinch of dried ground cloves

1 cinnamon stick
300ml/½ pint orange juice
3 tbsp thin-cut orange marmalade
½ lemon

1   Put all the dried fruit into the slow cooker and add the cloves and cinnamon stick. Stir in the orange juice, marmalade and 1 litre/1¾ pints cold water. Make sure the fruit is pushed down under the surface of the liquid (apple rings tend to float so you may need to put them at the bottom and weigh them down with other fruit).

2   Cut the lemon into thin slices and float them on top of the liquid.

3   Cover with the lid and cook on Low for 6–10 hours.

4   Stir gently before serving.

CHOCOLATE & LIME PANCAKES

Wickedly tempting, definitely not for a day when you are counting calories. Basic pancakes can be made ahead; they also freeze well, but can now be found in many stores. Wonderful with maple syrup for brunch, or cut into small portions and serve with scoops of vanilla ice cream or even custard for dinner.

SERVES 6–8	Butter, for greasing	6 ready-made pancakes
	1 lime	Maple syrup, to serve
HIGH 1½–2½ hours	8 tbsp nutty chocolate spread	
	200g/7 oz light cream cheese	

1   Preheat the slow cooker on High while you prepare the ingredients.

2   Lightly grease and line the base of a deep 18cm/7 inch ovenproof dish with non-stick baking paper. (Check the dish fits inside your slow cooker.) Lightly grease another disc of non-stick baking paper for the top. Put the kettle on to boil.

3   Finely grate the rind from half the lime. Cut the lime in half and squeeze out the juice (about 2 tbsp).

4   Spoon the nutty chocolate spread into a bowl and stir in the cream cheese, lime rind and juice.

5   Spread some of the chocolate filling over five of the pancakes, taking it almost to the edges. Layer the topped pancakes in the prepared dish; the edges will curl a little up the sides of the dish. Top with the remaining pancake and gently press the paper disc on top, buttered side down.

6   Cover the dish tightly with foil and put into the slow cooker. Pour in sufficient hot water to come half-way up the sides of the dish. Cover with the lid and cook on High for 1½–2½ hours until hot.

7   Lift out of the slow cooker, remove the foil and paper disc and loosen the edges with a knife. Turn onto a warm plate, cut into wedges and pour over maple syrup.

WARM FIGS WITH ORANGE, HONEY & WALNUTS

To serve this taste of the Mediterranean as a dessert, try adding a splash of sweet sherry or Italian Vin Santo with the orange juice in step 3 and then accompany the warm figs with mascarpone cheese, whipped double cream or vanilla ice cream. Any left over can be chilled and served later.

SERVES 4–6

HIGH 1–1½ hours

8 large fresh ripe figs
Butter for greasing
100g/3½ oz walnut pieces
3 tbsp clear honey, plus extra to serve

100ml/3½ fl oz orange juice
Thick Greek yogurt, to serve

1 Trim the stalks off the figs and cut each one into quarters without cutting all the way through the base. Gently squeeze the bottom of each fruit to open it out, flower like.

2 Lightly butter the inside of the slow cooker. Arrange the figs, upright and in a single layer, in it.

3 Roughly chop the walnuts and stir them with the honey. Put a small spoonful of the mixture into the centre of each fruit. Drizzle the orange juice over the figs.

4 Cover with the lid and cook on High for 1–1½ hours until the figs are soft and warmed through.

5 Carefully lift out into a serving dish and spoon the juices over the top. Serve with a generous spoonful of Greek yogurt and, if liked, extra honey drizzled over the top.

Hot Muesli with Cranberries & Blueberries

A hot mix of cereals, grains and fruits. Don't reserve just for breakfast. A healthy bowl of muesli is good any time of the day and can also be eaten cold. Serve with milk or yogurt. Put in a container and take for lunch. For extra crunch, scatter over a handful of chopped walnuts.

SERVES 6–8

LOW 8–10 hours

70g/2½ oz whole oat grains
50g/1¾ oz millet seeds
50g/1¾ oz wheat or barley flakes
40g/1½ oz sultanas

40g/1½ oz dried blueberries
40g/1½ oz dried cranberries
½ tsp ground cinnamon

1 Put all the ingredients into the slow cooker.

2 Pour over 1 litre/1¾ pints cold water and stir well.

3 Cover with the lid and cook on Low for 8–10 hours until the grains are soft and the dried fruits are soft and beginning to collapse.

4 Stir gently before serving.

RICE WITH SMOKED HADDOCK

Based on the traditional breakfast dish called Kedgeree, this also makes a great supper dish. For the best flavour use non-dyed haddock.

SERVES 6	1 medium onion	2 tsp fish or vegetable bouillon powder
	250g/9 oz easy-cook basmati or easy-cook	Small handful of parsley
HIGH 1 hour	long grain rice	1 lemon
+ 30 minutes	3 medium eggs	Salt and freshly milled pepper
	About 500g/1 lb 2 oz smoked haddock	
	85g/3 oz butter	

1 Preheat the slow cooker on High.

2 Finely chop the onion. Wash and drain the rice. Wrap each egg individually in foil. Wrap the smoked haddock securely in foil, cutting it into manageable-size pieces if necessary and arranging it in an even layer.

3 Heat the butter in a saucepan on the hob and add the onion. Cook over medium heat for about 8 minutes, stirring occasionally, until softened and just beginning to turn golden brown.

4 Stir the rice into the onion, and then add 700ml/1¼ pints water and the bouillon powder. Bring just to the boil, stir well and pour the mixture into the slow cooker.

5 Push the foil-wrapped eggs into the rice and lay the parcel of fish on top.

6 Cover with the lid and cook on High for 1 hour.

7 Lift out the four foil packets and put to one side. Gently stir the rice, replace the lid and continue cooking for a further 30 minutes until the rice has absorbed the liquid.

8 Meanwhile, flake the fish, removing all skin and bones but reserving any juices. Unwrap the eggs, remove their shells and chop or cut into slices or wedges. Finely chop the parsley. Cut the lemon into wedges.

9 Just before serving, stir the fish and its juices into the rice and add the parsley and seasoning to taste.

10 Top the rice with the egg slices/wedges and serve with lemon wedges for squeezing over.

Courgette & Mushroom Frittata

Firmer than an omelette, frittatas are delicious hot or cold and would make a good picnic dish. Serve with hot toast or salad.

SERVES 4	25g/1 oz butter plus small piece for greasing	2 tbsp milk
	2 shallots	1 tsp pepper sauce (optional)
HIGH 1½–2½ hours	1 garlic clove	2 tbsp fresh thyme leaves
	1 medium courgette	Freshly milled salt and black pepper
	100g/3½ oz button mushrooms	2 tsp olive oil
	8 medium eggs	

1　Preheat the slow cooker on High while you prepare the ingredients.

2　Lightly grease and line the base of an 18cm/7 inch deep ovenproof dish with non-stick baking paper. (Check the dish fits inside your slow cooker.) Put the kettle on to boil.

3　Finely chop the shallots and garlic. Finely grate the courgette and thinly slice the mushrooms. Break the eggs into a bowl and stir in the milk, pepper sauce (if using), thyme leaves and a little seasoning.

4　Heat the butter and oil in a pan and fry the shallots and garlic for 5 minutes until softened. Stir in the courgette and mushrooms and cook for a further 5 minutes.

5　Remove from the heat, stir in the egg mixture and tip into the prepared dish.

6　Put the dish into the slow cooker. Pour in sufficient hot water to come half-way up the sides of the dish. Cover with the lid and cook on High for 1½–2½ hours until set and cooked through.

7　Lift the dish out of the slow cooker and loosen the edges with a knife. Turn onto a warm plate, cut into wedges and serve hot or cold.

DEVILLED FRANKFURTERS, GAMMON & SMOKED SAUSAGE

Hot and spicy, certainly a wake-you-up dish for the morning. Cayenne pepper is hot, so measure carefully. Serve with lots of hot buttered toast.

SERVES 6–8

HIGH 1½–2½ hours

1 medium red onion
400g/14 oz button mushrooms
400g/14 oz cherry tomatoes
8 frankfurter sausages
250g/9 oz smoked sausage
250g/9 oz smoked gammon
1 tbsp olive oil

2 tbsp Worcestershire sauce
3 tbsp wholegrain mustard
½ tsp cayenne pepper
1 tbsp chicken bouillon powder
Freshly milled black pepper
Chopped fresh parsley, to serve

1   Preheat the slow cooker on High while you prepare the ingredients.

2   Put the kettle on to boil. Finely chop the onion. Slice the mushrooms and tomatoes in half. Cut each frankfurter into three, slice the smoked sausage and dice the gammon.

3   Heat a large non-stick pan, add the sausages and gammon and fry for a few minutes until lightly browned. Transfer to the slow cooker.

4   If necessary add a little of the oil to the pan and heat. Add the onion and cook for 5 minutes until softened. Stir in the Worcestershire sauce, mustard, cayenne, bouillon powder and a little seasoning. Pour over 300ml/½ pint hot water and bring just to the boil. Stir in the mushrooms and tomatoes and tip over the meat in the slow cooker.

5   Cover with the lid and cook on High for 1½–2½ hours until piping hot and cooked through. Serve sprinkled with a generous amount of parsley.

3. Slow Soups

Diverse and delicious, all these soup recipes are perfect for your slow cooker. You will find here soups for every day and soups for smart occasions, soups as starters and some that are ideal as main courses. Some soups are chunky and others, after whizzing them with your hand-held stick blender, will produce a silkier, smoother result.

Slow cooking gives soups an extra dimension. The ingredients gently interact, producing complex and satisfying flavours which will delight the taste buds as well as being wholesome and nutritious fare. And there are always those last-minute additions to each bowl as it is served – some crusty bread, a handful of olives, a swirl of cream or yogurt or a handful of fresh herbs.

Tomato, Basil & Rice Soup

Add the rice of your choice – brown, basmati or wild rice are all good. For a lighter soup, perhaps to serve as a starter, simply omit the rice and serve the soup with crisp-fried croûtons.

SERVES 6	1 large red onion	Salt and freshly milled pepper
	2 garlic cloves	1 chicken stock cube
LOW 6–8 hours	500g/1 lb 2 oz fresh ripe tomatoes	1 generous tsp vegetable bouillon powder
+ 20–30 minutes	400g can whole plum tomatoes	Generous handful of fresh basil leaves
	1 tbsp sugar	250g packet of ready-cooked rice
	1 tbsp tomato purée	Extra virgin olive oil, to serve

1   Preheat the slow cooker on High while you prepare the ingredients.

2   Put the kettle on to boil. Finely chop the onion and garlic. Roughly chop the fresh tomatoes.

3   Put the onion, garlic and fresh tomatoes into the slow cooker. Add the can of tomatoes, chopping them roughly as you tip them in, and the sugar, tomato purée and a little seasoning.

4   Dissolve the stock cube and bouillon powder in 1.2 litres/2 pints boiling water (from the kettle) and pour into the slow cooker.

5   Cover with the lid and cook on Low for 6–8 hours.

6   About 30 minutes before serving, add the basil leaves and, with a hand-held stick blender, whizz until very smooth. Adjust the seasoning to taste and stir in the rice.

7   Replace the lid and continue cooking on Low for 20–30 minutes.

8   Ladle into warmed bowls and drizzle each serving with a little olive oil.

SWEET POTATO & CHICKPEA SOUP

This fat-free soup couldn't be easier to make. If you like spicy flavours, use a hot mango chutney. We like to serve this soup fairly chunky but you can blend it until smooth if you wish (see step 6).

SERVES 6	2 sweet potatoes, total weight about 600g/1 lb 5 oz	1 chicken stock cube
	1 potato, about 175g/6 oz	1 generous tsp vegetable bouillon powder
LOW 7–10 hours	1 red onion	2 tbsp mango chutney
	1 medium carrot	Salt and freshly milled black pepper
	1 garlic clove	Small handful of fresh coriander leaves (optional)
	410g can chickpeas in water	

1   Preheat the slow cooker on High while you prepare the ingredients.

2   Put the kettle on to boil. Chop the sweet potatoes and potato into small pieces. Finely chop the onion, carrot and garlic.

3   Put all the chopped vegetables into the slow cooker. Add the chickpeas, including their water.

4   Dissolve the stock cube and bouillon powder in 1.2 litres/2 pints boiling water (from the kettle) and stir into the slow cooker.

5   Cover with the lid and cook on Low for 7–10 hours.

6   Add the mango chutney and, with a hand-held stick blender, whizz to a thick (but not entirely smooth – see note above) texture.

7   Season to taste and serve with coriander leaves scattered over, if using.

CHICKEN CHOWDER

A thick, rich, chunky mixture based on the famous American soup. Serve with hot, crusty bread.

SERVES 6	4 boneless, skinless chicken thighs	25g/1 oz butter
	2 boneless, skinless chicken breasts	2 chicken stock cubes
LOW 6–8 hours	1 large onion	1 generous tsp vegetable bouillon powder
	1 large potato	1 small red pepper
	1 large carrot	175g can sweetcorn kernels
	4 celery sticks	Salt and freshly milled pepper
	1 tbsp olive oil	50ml/¼ pint double cream

1   Preheat the slow cooker on High while you prepare the ingredients.

2   Trim and cut the chicken into small pieces. Chop the onion, potato, carrot and celery into fairly small pieces.

3   Heat the oil and butter in a large saucepan on the hob. Add the onion, potato, carrot and celery and cook over medium-high heat for 5–8 minutes, stirring occasionally, until beginning to soften.

4   Stir the chicken into the vegetables and cook quickly for 2–3 minutes until the contents of the pan just begin to turn golden brown. Add the stock cubes and bouillon powder and stir in 1.2 litres/2 pints water. Bring just to the boil and tip the mixture into the slow cooker.

5   Cover with the lid and cook on Low for 6–8 hours until the vegetables and chicken are very tender.

6   Meanwhile, halve the red pepper, remove and discard the seeds and stalk, and slice thinly. Drain the sweetcorn.

7   About 30 minutes before serving, add the red pepper and sweetcorn, adjust the seasoning to taste, and stir in the cream. Replace the lid and continue cooking on Low for 20–30 minutes.

BORLOTTI BEAN SOUP WITH SPICY SAUSAGE

You will need to soak the dried beans overnight before cooking. Alternatively, use two or three 400g cans of beans, drained and added in step 3. For a vegetarian version, add extra vegetable bouillon powder in place of the chicken stock cube and serve the soup topped with grated cheese instead of the sausage.

SERVES 6	250g/9 oz dried borlotti beans	400g can chopped tomatoes
	1 onion	1 chicken stock cube
LOW 7–10 hours	1 carrot	1 generous tsp vegetable bouillon powder
	2 celery sticks	Salt and freshly milled black pepper
	2 garlic cloves	About 150g/5½ oz spicy sausage, such as chorizo
	1 tbsp olive oil	Crusty bread, to serve

1 Soak the borlotti beans in plenty of cold water for at least 8 hours or overnight. Next day, drain the beans and put into a large saucepan on the hob. Cover well with water and boil rapidly for 10 minutes.

2 Preheat the slow cooker on High while you prepare the rest of the ingredients.

3 Drain the boiled beans and put them into the slow cooker. Finely chop the onion, carrot, celery and garlic.

4 Put the chopped vegetables into a large saucepan with the oil and cook over medium heat for 5–10 minutes until slightly softened and beginning to turn golden brown. Add the tomatoes, chicken stock cube, bouillon powder and 1.5 litres/2¾ pints water. Bring just to the boil and tip over the beans in the slow cooker.

5 Cover with the lid and cook on Low for 7–10 hours until the beans are tender.

6 Season to taste with salt and pepper.

7 Cut the sausage into thin slices and divide between warmed serving bowls. Ladle the soup over the top and serve with crusty bread.

Potato, Leek & Smoked Ham Soup with Olives

A substantial soup which definitely could be eaten as a main meal. Do use smoked ham if possible; it adds its own distinctive flavour.

SERVES 4–6

LOW 6–8 hours

2 leeks
1 large onion
1 or 2 potatoes, weighing about 350g/12 oz
200g/7 oz smoked ham
8 stoned black olives

1 tsp olive oil
2 tbsp vegetable bouillon powder
3 tbsp wholegrain mustard
Freshly milled salt and black pepper
Crusty brown bread, to serve

1   Preheat the slow cooker on High while you prepare the ingredients.

2   Put the kettle on to boil. Thinly slice the leeks and finely chop the onion. Leave the potato skins on and finely chop. Cut the ham into small dice. Quarter the olives.

3   Heat the oil in a large pan and fry the leeks and onion for about 3 minutes until softened. Add the potatoes and cook for a further 5 minutes until lightly browned.

4   Stir the ham, bouillon powder, mustard and a little seasoning into the pan and pour over 1 litre/1¾ pints boiling water. Bring just to the boil and pour into the slow cooker.

5   Cover with the lid and cook on Low for 6–8 hours. Use a potato masher to partially crush the vegetables. Stir in the olive quarters and serve with crusty brown bread.

THAI CURRY SOUP WITH PORK, CHILLI & LEMON GRASS

Full of oriental flavours this soup is mildly hot. For a hotter version use a few of the chilli seeds. Lemon grass is a traditional flavour in Thai cooking. It looks rather like a dry spring onion – available fresh, dry or in jars.

SERVES 4–6	6 spring onions	1 tbsp green Thai curry paste
	1 garlic clove	150ml/¼ pint coconut milk
LOW 6–8 hours	1 stem lemon grass	1 tbsp lime juice
	Small piece of fresh root ginger	2 tbsp chicken bouillon powder
	1 red chilli (see page 14)	Freshly milled black pepper
	150g/5½ oz minced lean pork	4 tbsp freshly chopped coriander

1   Preheat the slow cooker on High while you prepare the ingredients.

2   Put the kettle on to boil. Finely slice the spring onions and crush the garlic. Cut the lemon grass vertically in half. Coarsely grate the root ginger. Cut the chilli in half, remove and discard the seeds and stalk, and finely chop.

3   Heat a wide non-stick pan, and when hot tip in the minced pork and cook for about 5 minutes until lightly brown, stirring and breaking up the meat with a wooden spoon. Add the spring onions, garlic, lemon grass, ginger and chilli and cook for a further 2–3 minutes.

4   Stir in the curry paste, coconut milk, lime juice, bouillon powder and a little seasoning. Pour over 1 litre/1¾ pints boiling water. Heat until bubbles begin to rise to the surface. Pour into the slow cooker.

5   Cover with the lid and cook on Low for 6–8 hours. Stir in the coriander just before serving.

GREEN LENTIL & APPLE SOUP

Green lentils don't require soaking before they are cooked. For a smooth soup whizz until smooth with a stick blender before you add the spinach leaves. The recipe makes a generous quantity, so could be a main meal.

SERVES 4–6	200g/7 oz green Puy lentils	1 tbsp vegetable bouillon powder
	1 large red onion	4 sage leaves
LOW 5–7 hours	1 garlic clove	1 bay leaf
+ 30 minutes	3 green eating apples	Freshly milled salt and black pepper
	100g/3½ oz young spinach leaves	Hot pitta breads, to serve
	1 tbsp olive oil	

1   Preheat the slow cooker on High while you prepare the ingredients.

2   Put the kettle on to boil. Wash the lentils in plenty of cold water and drain. Finely chop the onion and garlic. Quarter the apples, remove and discard the cores, and cut into small pieces. Wash the spinach leaves.

3   Heat the oil in a large pan and fry the chopped onion and garlic for about 3 minutes. Add the chopped apples and cook for a further 2–3 minutes until lightly browned.

4   Stir the drained lentils, bouillon powder, sage leaves and bay leaf into the pan and pour over 1.5 litres/2¾ pints boiling water. Bring just to the boil and pour into the slow cooker.

5   Cover with the lid and cook on Low for 5–7 hours until the lentils are cooked and soft.

6   Remove the lid and with a slotted spoon lift out the bay leaf. Use a stick blender to whizz the soup smooth and season if necessary. Stir in the spinach leaves, cover again with the lid and cook for a further 30 minutes. Stir and serve with hot pitta breads.

FENNEL & RED PEPPER SOUP WITH TAMARIND & MINT

Tamarind is a date-like fruit growing in pods. This sour-and-sweet pulp (available as a paste) is so versatile for adding its concentrated flavour to full-bodied dishes. Here it complements the aniseed flavour of fennel and peppers.

SERVES 4–6	2 medium fennel bulbs	1 tsp lemon oil
	2 red peppers	1 tbsp lemon juice
LOW 6–8 hours	4 spring onions	1 tbsp tamarind paste
	1 garlic clove	Handful of mint sprigs
	1 litre/1¾ pints vegetable stock	

1   Preheat the slow cooker on High while you prepare the ingredients.

2   Trim the fennel bulbs and finely chop. Cut the peppers in half, remove and discard their seeds and stalks, and slice thinly. Chop the spring onions and crush the garlic.

3   Put all the ingredients into the slow cooker and stir thoroughly.

4   Cover with the lid and cook on Low for 6–8 hours until the vegetables are tender and soft.

4. FAMILIES UNWIND

ONCE UPON A TIME, families used to sit down together to share their main meal of the day. For many of us, this is still an ideal, but how often does it actually happen? For all sorts of reasons (shift work, school, clubs, gym, French classes) we resort instead to hurriedly prepared food and unsatisfactory snacks, and often we eat alone. This is where slow cooking comes into its own.

From your slow cooker the same specially prepared meal can be eaten by everyone in the family, whether separately or together, throughout the evening. The food, once cooked, stays hot and ready to serve. So you can go out to work in the morning knowing that an exciting and energy-saving dish awaits the family at supper-time.

Many of these recipes would be suitable for freezing, especially if the ingredients are doubled in quantity. So, as an added bonus, you can eat some straight away and save the rest for another day.

HONEYED CHICKEN

Use a chicken which is a snug fit. Herbs and spices impart flavour to the bird.

SERVES 4–6	2 large red onions	2 tbsp unsweetened orange juice
	A large chicken, weighing about 2.25kg/5 lb	4 tbsp freshly chopped parsley
LOW 8–10 hours	2 tbsp set honey	Freshly milled salt and pepper
	100g/3½ oz butter	6 rosemary sprigs
	2 tbsp wholegrain mustard	600ml/1 pint chicken stock

1   Preheat the slow cooker on High while you prepare the ingredients.

2   Finely chop the onions. If the chicken has been trussed, remove and discard the string and any excess fat from inside the body cavity. From the neck end push your fingers between the skin and flesh to make a cavity over the breast and the top of the legs.

3   In a small bowl mix together the honey, butter, mustard, orange juice, parsley and a little seasoning.

4   Place the chicken on a large plate or board and push the rosemary sprigs into the body cavity. Tilt the chicken with the neck end uppermost then spoon the honey mixture under the skin. With your fingers press and smooth the mixture evenly over the breast and legs. Don't worry if any flows out.

5   Scatter the chopped onion over the base of the slow cooker. Put the chicken on top, spooning over any excess honey mixture. Pour over the stock. Cover with the lid and cook on Low for 8–10 hours until the chicken is cooked through and almost falling off the bone.

6   With slotted spoons carefully lift the chicken onto a large plate, cover and keep warm. With a stick blender whizz the sauce until smooth.

7   Cut the chicken into portions and serve with the sauce poured over.

"Hunter's" Chicken

Based on the Italian dish Chicken Cacciatore, with chicken, tomatoes, onions, mushrooms, all cooked in white wine. Instead of wine, you could use cider or stock. Serve with crusty bread, couscous, polenta or mashed potatoes.

SERVES 6

LOW 4–6 hours

2 tbsp plain flour
Salt and freshly milled black pepper
12 chicken thighs
2 medium onions
1 large red pepper
2 garlic cloves

150g/5½ oz mushrooms
1 tbsp olive oil
400g can chopped tomatoes
300ml/½ pint dry white wine
Few sprigs of fresh thyme

1   Preheat the slow cooker on High while you prepare the ingredients.

2   Season the flour with salt and pepper. Trim the chicken thighs of any excess skin and fat. Toss the chicken in the seasoned flour until well coated (we find this easiest to do in a large plastic food bag). Thinly slice the onions and red pepper, finely chop the garlic cloves and thickly slice the mushrooms.

3   Heat a large non-stick frying pan on the hob. When hot add the oil and half the chicken pieces, skin side down. Cook over high heat until the skin is golden brown and crisp. Lift out and set aside. Repeat with the remaining chicken.

4   Put the onions and pepper into the hot pan and cook over medium-high heat for about 5 minutes, stirring occasionally, until beginning to soften and turn golden brown. Add the garlic, mushrooms, tomatoes, wine and thyme. Bring just to the boil and transfer to the slow cooker.

5   Arrange the chicken pieces on top, skin side up, in an even layer and push them down gently into the vegetables.

6   Cover with the lid and cook on Low for 4–6 hours until the chicken and vegetables are very tender.

CURRIED TURKEY & SWEET POTATO LAYER

This dish is equally good made with beef, pork or lamb mince in place of turkey.

SERVES 4–6	700g/1 lb 9 oz sweet potatoes	2 tbsp mild curry paste
	1 large red onion	2 tbsp tomato purée
LOW 6–8 hours	2 garlic cloves	300ml/½ pint passata
	Small bunch of coriander	200g/7 oz garden peas
	1 tbsp olive oil	Freshly milled salt and black pepper
	1 tbsp cumin seeds	1 tbsp chicken bouillon powder
	600g/1 lb 5 oz turkey mince	Extra chopped fresh coriander, to serve

1 Preheat the slow cooker on High while you prepare the ingredients.

2 Put the kettle on to boil. Peel and thinly slice the sweet potatoes. Finely chop the onion and garlic. Roughly chop the coriander.

3 Heat the oil in a wide non-stick pan and cook the cumin seeds for 1–2 seconds until they 'pop', immediately spoon onto kitchen paper. Add the onion and garlic to the pan and cook for 5 minutes until softened then add the minced turkey and cook for about 5 minutes until lightly brown, stirring and breaking up the meat with a wooden spoon. Stir in the coriander, cumin seeds, curry paste, tomato purée, passata, peas and a little seasoning. Mix thoroughly and remove from the heat. Put the bouillon powder in a jug and pour over 700ml/1¼ pints hot water.

4 Carefully scatter a third of the sliced potatoes in the base of the slow cooker pot. Cover with half of the turkey mix, repeat with the potato and meat mixture, ending with a layer of potato. Press down with the back of a spoon. Pour over the stock and cover with the lid.

5 Cook on Low for 6–8 hours. Sprinkle over extra coriander just before serving.

BEEF WITH RED WINE, GARLIC & THYME

Long slow cooking tenderises meat joints and allows flavours to develop. Melting and succulent, the meat starts to fall apart.

SERVES 6–8

LOW 8–10 hours

A boned, rolled joint of brisket, weighing about
   1.25kg/2¾ lb
3 medium onions
2 medium carrots
2 garlic cloves
150ml/¼ pint beef stock

450ml/16 fl oz red wine
1 tbsp wholegrain mustard
A few thyme sprigs
1 bay leaf
1 tsp freshly milled black pepper

1   Preheat the slow cooker on High while you prepare the ingredients.

2   Trim any excess fat from the joint of brisket. Finely chop the onions, thinly slice the carrots and crush the garlic.

3   Heat a large wide pan, and when hot add the brisket and brown quickly on all sides. Carefully lift into the slow cooker.

4   Tip the onions into the pan and cook for about 5 minutes until lightly browned, stirring occasionally.

5   Add the remaining ingredients to the browned onions and heat until bubbles begin to rise to the surface. Pour into the slow cooker over the meat.

6   Cover with the lid and cook on Low for 8–10 hours until the meat is tender and almost falling apart.

7   With slotted spoons carefully lift the brisket onto a large plate, cover and keep warm. Lift out and discard the woody thyme stalks and bay leaf. If you prefer a thicker sauce, use a stick blender and whizz until smooth.

8   Slice or tear the meat into pieces and serve with the sauce spooned over.

BEEF & PORK MEAT LOAF

This 'loaf' is cooked in a round cake tin. Tasty hot or cold. Serve with salad, pickles and tiny hot potatoes.

SERVES 6–8	Oil, for greasing	350g/12 oz lean minced beef
	1 small red onion	150g/5½ oz lean minced pork
HIGH 4–6 hours	1 garlic clove	60g/2¼ oz fresh breadcrumbs
	1 red eating apple	2 tbsp redcurrant jelly
	Small bunch of parsley	2 medium eggs
	4 sage leaves	Freshly milled salt and black pepper

1   Preheat the slow cooker on High while you prepare the ingredients.

2   Lightly grease and line the base of an 18cm/7 inch deep ovenproof dish with non-stick baking paper. Put the kettle on to boil. Finely chop the onion and garlic. Cut the apple into quarters, remove the cores and grate the fruit coarsely (there's no need to peel the apple). Finely chop the parsley and sage.

3   Heat a wide non-stick pan, and when hot tip in the minced beef and pork and cook for about 5 minutes until lightly brown, stirring and breaking up the meat with a wooden spoon. With a slotted spoon remove the mince and put on a plate. Add the onion and garlic to the pan and cook for 5 minutes until softened. Return the mince to the pan and stir in the apple and herbs.

4   Remove from the heat, cool for a few minutes and stir in the breadcrumbs, redcurrant jelly, eggs and seasoning. Spoon into the prepared dish.

5   Cover the dish tightly with foil and put into the slow cooker. Pour in sufficient hot water to come half-way up the sides of the dish. Cover with the lid and cook on High for 4–6 hours.

6   Lift the dish out of the slow cooker and leave to stand for 10 minutes. Loosen the edges with a knife and carefully turn out. Serve hot or cold, cut into slices.

LEG OF LAMB WITH RED WINE & LENTILS

Choose a lamb joint that will fit your slow cooker – we usually ask our butcher to trim off the knuckle end of the leg. Serve with potatoes and a green salad or freshly cooked vegetables of your choice.

SERVES 6	200g/7 oz green lentils	1 tbsp olive oil
	1 medium onion	1.5kg/3¼ lb leg of lamb
LOW 6–9 hours	1 medium carrot	400g can chopped tomatoes
	2 celery sticks	400ml/14 fl oz red wine
	2 garlic cloves	2 bay leaves
	A few fresh rosemary leaves	Salt and freshly ground black pepper

1. Put the lentils into a saucepan on the hob, cover well with water and boil rapidly for 10 minutes.

2. Preheat the slow cooker on High while you prepare the rest of the ingredients.

3. Drain the boiled lentils and put them into the slow cooker. Finely chop the onion, carrot, celery and garlic. Finely chop the rosemary – you will need about a teaspoonful.

4. Heat a large non-stick frying pan on the hob. When hot add the oil and brown the lamb quickly on all sides. Lift out onto a plate.

5. Add the onion, carrot, celery and garlic to the hot pan and cook over medium heat for 5–10 minutes until softened and just beginning to turn golden brown. Add the tomatoes, wine, rosemary, bay leaves and seasoning. Bring just to the boil and pour over the lentils in the slow cooker. Add the lamb and its juices and push it gently so that it nestles into the lentils.

6. Cover with the lid and cook on Low for 6–9 hours until the lamb and lentils are tender.

7. To serve, transfer the lamb to a warmed plate and carve. Taste the lentils and adjust the seasoning if necessary. Serve with the lamb.

LAMB MEATBALLS IN TOMATO SAUCE

Serve with freshly cooked rice or spaghetti.

SERVES 6	**Meatballs:**	**Sauce:**
	1 large onion	1 small onion
LOW 4–6 hours	2 garlic cloves	1 small carrot
	Small handful of fresh mint leaves	1 celery stick
	Small handful of fresh parsley	1 tbsp olive oil
	1 large egg	400g can chopped tomatoes
	800g/1¾ lb lean minced lamb	300ml/½ pint vegetable or chicken stock
	100g/3½ oz fresh breadcrumbs	1 tbsp tomato purée
	1½ tsp ground cumin	1 tbsp sugar
	Salt and freshly milled black pepper	Salt and freshly milled black pepper
	Olive oil	

1   To make the meatballs, finely chop the onion, garlic, mint and parsley. Lightly beat the egg. In a large mixing bowl, combine all the ingredients except the oil. Using wetted hands, shape the mixture into about 30 balls.

2   Preheat the slow cooker. Finely chop the onion, carrot and celery.

3   Heat a large non-stick frying pan on the hob. When hot, add a little oil and half the meatballs in a single layer. Cook quickly until golden brown all over. Transfer to the slow cooker and repeat with the remaining meatballs.

4   Add the oil to the hot frying pan with the onion, carrot and celery. Cook for about 5 minutes until golden brown. Stir in the remaining ingredients, bring just to the boil and pour the mixture over the meatballs in the slow cooker.

5   Cover with the lid and cook on Low for 4–6 hours.

TRADITIONAL BAKED BEANS WITH PORK

Haricot or navy beans are often used in recipes for traditional Boston baked beans. A piece of pork or bacon added to the beans is traditional and gives a depth of flavour. Serve with hot crusty bread.

SERVES 6–8	500g/1 lb 2 oz haricot beans	2 tbsp dark brown sugar
	250g/9 oz pork or bacon	2 tsp mustard powder
LOW 8–10 hours	3 large onions	4 tbsp molasses (black treacle)
	150ml/¼ pint passata	1 tsp freshly milled black pepper
	2 tbsp vegetable bouillon powder	

1   Soak the beans overnight in plenty of cold water, or, alternatively, boil them in plenty of water for 2 minutes and leave to absorb the liquid for 2 hours.

2   Preheat the slow cooker on High while you prepare the ingredients.

3   Put the kettle on to boil. Trim excess fat from the pork or the rind from the bacon. Finely chop the onions. Drain the beans.

4   Heat a non-stick pan and when hot add the pork or bacon and brown quickly on all sides. Lift out with a slotted spoon.

5   Stir the remaining ingredients into the pan and pour over 700ml/1¼ pints boiling water. Bring back to the boil and cook for 10 minutes.

6   Transfer to the slow cooker and push the pork or bacon into the middle of the mixture. With the back of a spoon push the beans just under the liquid.

7   Cover with the lid and cook on Low for 8–10 hours until the meat is tender and the beans cooked through.

8   With a slotted spoon lift out the meat, cut into small pieces and return to the slow cooker. Stir and serve.

Sweet & Sour Pork

Serve with plenty of freshly cooked rice and perhaps a green salad. Any left over can be frozen for another time and reheated gently in a pan on the hob.

SERVES 6–8	1.4kg/3 lb lean pork	4 tbsp light soy sauce
	2 medium onions	2 tbsp red or white wine vinegar
LOW 5–8 hours	2 garlic cloves	2 tbsp sugar
	2 tbsp olive oil	Salt and freshly milled black pepper
	250g can crushed pineapple	3 tbsp cornflour
	1 chicken stock cube	150ml/¼ pint dry sherry

1   Preheat the slow cooker while you prepare the ingredients.

2   Trim the pork and cut into large bite-size pieces. Slice the onions and finely chop the garlic.

3   Heat a large non-stick frying pan on the hob. When hot, add 1 tbsp oil and the onions. Cook over medium heat for 5–10 minutes until beginning to soften and turn golden brown. Stir in the garlic and transfer to the slow cooker.

4   Add the remaining 1 tbsp oil to the pan and brown the pork quickly in batches and transfer it to the slow cooker.

5   To the hot frying pan add 500ml/18 fl oz water and the pineapple (including its juice), stock cube, soy sauce, vinegar, sugar and seasoning. While it heats, gradually blend the cornflour with the sherry to make a smooth paste and add to the pan. Stirring continuously, bring to the boil. Pour the thickened sauce over the contents of the slow cooker and stir well.

6   Cover with the lid and cook on Low for 5–8 hours until very tender. Stir gently before serving.

SLOW-COOKED GAMMON

Use smoked or unsmoked gammon, as preferred, and you may like to soak the joint overnight in plenty of cold water first to help remove any excess salt. Serve it hot with boiled and buttered new potatoes and a tomato-and-onion salad. Or serve it cold as part of a buffet or Ploughman's Lunch, or sliced in sandwiches and salads. Once the gammon is cooked, you could glaze it by removing its rind, sprinkling the fat side with demerara sugar and browning quickly under a hot grill. The cooking juices could be made into a sauce by transferring them to a saucepan on the hob and blending in some cornflour, adjusting the seasoning to taste and adding a handful of finely chopped fresh parsley last minute.

SERVES 6–8

LOW 4–6 hours

1 large onion	6 black peppercorns
1 large carrot	4 whole cloves
2 celery sticks	2 bay leaves
1.8kg/4 lb gammon joint, soaked if wished (see note above) and drained	A few parsley stalks
	2 tbsp wholegrain mustard

1   Preheat the slow cooker while you prepare the ingredients.

2   Put the kettle on to boil. Thinly slice the onion, carrot and celery.

3   Put the gammon into the slow cooker and scatter the onions and celery around the sides. Add the peppercorns, cloves, bay leaves and parsley stalks.

4   Pour over about 400ml/14 fl oz boiling water (from the kettle) and stir in the mustard.

5   Cover with the lid and cook on Low for 4–6 hours.

5. RELAX WITH FRIENDS

WHEN ENTERTAINING FRIENDS you naturally want to rustle up something special by way of a feast. But how can you achieve this without being tied to the kitchen and ignoring your guests while you go quietly frantic?

Your secret weapon is your slow cooker. Slow cooking, for four, six, eight or more, lets you conjure up a dish with some wonderful, intense flavours and still gives you plenty of time to talk to your guests without a care in the world. Your friends might just wonder how you managed to feed them with so little apparent effort.

Even after a busy day your slow cooker makes it possible to invite friends round for dinner or supper. At weekends it is just the ticket for relaxed entertaining – good company and a delicious meal, enjoyed together at leisure.

CHICKEN & PRAWNS

This can easily be adjusted to serve six or eight, depending on the size of your slow cooker. Serve in shallow bowls with crusty bread for mopping up the juices.

SERVES 4	500g/1 lb 2 oz baby potatoes	2 tsp sugar
	2 celery sticks	4 chicken breasts
LOW 4–6 hours	2 medium leeks	Salt and freshly milled black pepper
	1 medium carrot	Small handful of sugar snap peas
	1 garlic clove	½ lemon
	4 anchovy fillets	Small handful of baby spinach leaves
	400g can whole plum tomatoes	About 200g/7 oz cooked shelled king prawns, with
	1 chicken stock cube	tails on
	2 tbsp Worcestershire sauce	Extra virgin olive oil

1   Preheat the slow cooker on High while you prepare the ingredients.

2   Put the kettle on to boil. Thinly slice the potatoes, celery and the white parts of the leeks. Cut the carrot into small sticks. Finely chop the garlic and the anchovy fillets.

3   Put the prepared vegetables and anchovy fillets into the slow cooker and add the tomatoes, chopping them roughly as they go in. Dissolve the stock cube in 600ml/1 pint boiling water (from the kettle) and stir in the Worcestershire sauce and sugar. Pour the mixture over the contents of the slow cooker. Add the chicken breasts, pushing them down into the liquid. Season lightly.

4   Cover with the lid and cook on Low for 4–6 hours until the potatoes are tender.

5   Meanwhile, thinly slice the green leeks and thickly slice the sugar snap peas.

6   About 30 minutes before serving, adjust the seasoning to taste and squeeze in the juice from the lemon. Stir in the green leeks. Replace the lid and continue cooking for 20 minutes. Lift out the chicken and slice.

7   Stir in the chicken, sugar snap peas, spinach and prawns. Replace the lid and continue cooking for 10 minutes.

8   Drizzle a little olive oil over each serving.

Stuffed Shoulder of Lamb with Onion & Courgette Sauce

A succulent joint of meat with a caper, olive and walnut stuffing.

SERVES 6–8

LOW 6–8 hours

1 boned shoulder of lamb
3 large red onions
2 large garlic cloves
4 courgettes

Stuffing:
2 tbsp capers
10 stoned black olives
10 walnut halves
Large bunch of parsley
1 large lemon

75cl bottle dry white wine
150ml/¼ pint lamb or chicken stock
Freshly milled salt and black pepper

1   Preheat the slow cooker on High while you prepare the ingredients.

2   Trim excess fat from the shoulder of lamb. Finely chop the onions and crush the garlic. Chop the courgettes. Chop the capers, olives, walnuts and parsley. Finely grate the rind from the lemon, cut in half and squeeze out the juice.

3   Put half of the lemon rind and juice into a bowl and mix in the remaining stuffing ingredients. Put the meat, skin side down, and spread the stuffing over. Fold the meat over and tie with string to secure.

4   Heat a wide non-stick pan, brown the lamb on all sides and remove. Add the onions, garlic and courgettes. Cook for 5 minutes until starting to brown. Stir in the remaining lemon rind and juice, wine, stock and seasoning. Heat until almost bubbling.

5   Pour into the slow cooker and place the joint on top. Cover with the lid and cook on Low for 6–8 hours.

6   Lift the lamb onto a hot plate. With a stick-blender whizz the vegetables and liquid until smooth. Spoon the sauce onto hot plates and top with slices of lamb.

TWO-CHEESE FONDUE WITH CRISPY BACON

Here, everyone gathers around the slow cooker to dip crisp bread and vegetables into the creamy mixture of melted cheese and wine. If your slow cooker is a really large one, you may prefer to fondue ingredients in an ovenproof bowl, covered securely with foil. Stand it in the slow cooker and pour round sufficient boiling water (from the kettle) to come half-way up the sides of the dish and cook for the given time.

SERVES 6	300g/10½ oz Gruyère or Gouda cheese	To serve:
	300g/10½ oz Emmenthal cheese	Crusty bread
LOW 1–3 hours	1 large garlic clove	Vegetables, such as sticks of carrot, pepper and
	1 tbsp cornflour	cucumber; radishes, mange touts; wedges of Little
	300ml/½ pint dry white wine	Gem lettuce; chicory leaves
	Freshly grated nutmeg	
	Freshly milled white pepper	
	Few drops of chilli sauce	
	100g/3½ oz streaky bacon	

1   Preheat the slow cooker on High while you prepare the ingredients.

2   Grate the two cheeses. Cut the garlic clove in half and rub the cut sides over the inside of the slow cooker.

3   Put the grated cheeses into the slow cooker and stir in the cornflour. Add the white wine, a good pinch each of nutmeg and white pepper, and the chilli sauce. Stir well.

4   Cover with the lid and cook on Low for 1–3 hours.

5   Meanwhile, with scissors, trim the rind from the bacon rashers and cut into small strips. Put the bacon into a small non-stick frying pan and heat slowly until the fat begins to run. Increase the heat under the pan and cook quickly until the bacon is crisp and brown. Lift out onto kitchen paper to drain.

6   Just before serving, stir the crispy bacon pieces into the hot cheese mixture.

7   Serve with bread and vegetables for dipping.

SPICED LEG OF PORK COOKED IN CIDER

Meat cooked on the bone has lots of flavour. Long slow cooking means the meat will almost fall off the bone and is amazingly tender. Serve with noodles or sautéed potatoes.

SERVES 4–6	1 leg of pork, to fit your slow cooker	2 tsp ground cinnamon
	2 medium leeks	2 tsp ground ginger
LOW 6–8 hours	3 tart apples	150ml/¼ pint vegetable stock
	8 juniper berries	300ml/½ pint sweet cider
	2 tsp ground cloves	Freshly milled salt and black pepper

1   Preheat the slow cooker on High while you prepare the ingredients.

2   Put the kettle on to boil. Trim excess fat from the pork and with a sharp knife make deep slits all over the meat. Thinly slice the leeks. Cut the apples into quarters, remove the cores and chop the fruit (there's no need to peel the apples). Crush the juniper berries.

3   In a small bowl mix together the crushed juniper berries, ground cloves, cinnamon and ginger. Push this spice mix deep into the slits in the pork.

4   Heat a wide non-stick pan and cook the pork until golden brown on all sides.

5   Put the leeks and apples into the slow cooker and pour over the stock and cider and add a little seasoning. Put the pork on top and cover with the lid.

6   Cook on Low for 6–8 hours. Lift the meat onto a hot plate, it will almost fall apart. Serve with the leeks and apples and some of the liquid.

Game Terrine

This flavourful savoury mix could be used to make meatballs or burgers.

SERVES 4–6	600g/1 lb 5 oz skinned, boneless mixed game meat, such as venison, rabbit, pigeon or pheasant	1 tsp olive oil
		50g/1¾ oz rolled oats
HIGH 4–6 hours	2 rashers rindless smoked streaky bacon	8 juniper berries
	1 small red onion	1 tbsp whisky or milk
	1 garlic clove	100ml/3½ fl oz venison or chicken stock
	1 orange	1 medium egg
	Small bunch fresh parsley	¼ tsp freshly milled black pepper
	2 sage leaves	

1 Preheat the slow cooker on High while you prepare the ingredients. Cut a large sheet of non-stick baking paper and a large sheet of extra thick foil.

2 Finely chop the meat, bacon, onion and garlic. Grate the rind from half the orange, squeeze juice from the whole orange. Chop the parsley and sage.

3 Heat the oil in a wide non-stick pan, and cook the meat and bacon for about 5 minutes until lightly brown. With a slotted spoon remove and put in a large bowl. Add the onion and garlic to the pan and cook for 5 minutes until softened. Remove from the heat and stir in the oats. Tip into the bowl of meat and mix in the remaining ingredients.

4 Put the sheet of baking paper on a clean surface and spoon the filling down the centre. Form into an oblong shape. Wrap the paper tightly around the mixture and then double wrap in foil, making sure it is well sealed.

5 Put into the slow cooker. Pour in sufficient hot water to almost cover the foil package. Cover with the lid and cook on High for 4–6 hours.

6 Lift the parcel out of the slow cooker and stand for 10 minutes. Unwrap and slice.

SPANISH-STYLE RICE WITH CHICKEN, MUSSELS & PRAWNS

Based on the Spanish dish paella, in which saffron gives the rice its distinctive taste. This dish too is great for sharing with friends. A dressed green salad is the only accompaniment you may need.

SERVES 6	1 medium onion	1 generous tsp vegetable bouillon powder
	2 garlic cloves	500g/1 lb 2 oz easy-cook long grain rice
LOW 2–3 hours	1 red pepper	Freshly milled black pepper
	6 large chicken drumsticks	About 12 cooked mussels in their shells
	About 150g/5½ oz spicy sausage, such as chorizo	About 12 cooked, peeled king prawns, with tails on
	2 tbsp olive oil	Handful of frozen petits pois
	Pinch of saffron strands	2 ripe tomatoes
	1 chicken stock cube	Chopped fresh parsley, to garnish

1   Preheat the slow cooker on High.

2   Put the kettle on to boil. Finely chop the onion and garlic. Halve the pepper, remove and discard its seeds and stalk, and cut into thin strips. Trim the chicken of any excess skin and fat. Thinly slice the sausage.

3   Heat a large non-stick frying pan on the hob. When hot add the oil and the chicken drumsticks. Cook over medium to high heat until the skin is golden brown and crisp all over. Lift out and set aside.

4   Add the onion, pepper and garlic to the hot pan and cook over medium heat for about 5 minutes, stirring occasionally, until just beginning to soften. Stir in the saffron and sausage slices.

5   Dissolve the stock cube and bouillon powder in 1.2 litres/2 pints boiling water. Pour half the stock into the frying pan, bring just to the boil then transfer to the slow cooker. Stir in the remaining stock and rice. Season with black pepper. Add the browned chicken and its juices, gently pushing the pieces into the liquid.

6   Cover with the lid and cook on Low for 2–3 hours until the chicken is cooked through.

7   About 30 minutes before serving, stir in the mussels, prawns and petits pois.

8   Just before serving, finely chop the tomatoes and scatter them over the rice, together with some chopped parsley.

BAGNA CAUDA

We like to use the slow cooker to prepare things that often involve last-minute hassle – such as this rich anchovy and butter dish from Northern Italy. The mixture just sits there gently heating until we are ready to eat. Offer this dish as a starter or as a fun supper to share with friends – like a fondue, with bread and crudités.

SERVES 6	12 anchovy fillets in oil	To serve:
	4–6 garlic cloves	Plenty of crusty bread – offer a variety of types
LOW 1–3 hours	125g/4½ oz butter	Vegetables, such as sticks of carrot, pepper and
	250ml/9 fl oz extra virgin olive oil	cucumber; radishes, mange touts; wedges of Little
		Gem lettuce; chicory leaves

1   Preheat the slow cooker on High while you prepare the ingredients.

2   Put the kettle on to boil. Drain the anchovies and chop them into small pieces. Crush the garlic cloves. Cut the butter into small cubes.

3   Put the anchovies and garlic into an ovenproof bowl and stir in the olive oil and butter. Cover the dish securely with foil and stand it in the slow cooker. Pour in sufficient water to come half-way up the sides of the bowl.

4   Cover with the lid and cook on Low for 1–3 hours.

5   Using a whisk, stir the mixture well until thick and well mixed.

6   Serve with bread and vegetables for dipping.

CHILLI VENISON WITH CHOCOLATE

No one would guess there's chocolate in this rich venison dish, with hot chillies and the sharp fruity flavours of cranberries. Chocolate is often added to traditional Mexican dishes. In place of the spices, chillies and chocolate use a spoonful of chilli chocolate sauce (see page 182).

SERVES 6	900g/2 lb stewing venison	1 bay leaf
	3 rashers streaky bacon	1 cinnamon stick
LOW 6–8 hours	12 shallots or pickling onions	400ml/14 fl oz venison or chicken stock
	2 red chillies (see page 14)	150ml/¼ pint port or red wine
	150g/5½ oz cranberries	¼ tsp freshly milled black pepper
	¼ tsp ground nutmeg	55g/2 oz dark semi-sweet chocolate
	¼ tsp ground allspice	

1   Preheat the slow cooker on High while you prepare the ingredients.

2   Cut the venison into bite-sized pieces. With scissors snip the rinds from the bacon rashers and finely chop. Quarter the shallots or pickling onions. Cut the chillies in half, remove and discard their seeds and stalks, and slice thinly.

3   Put all the ingredients except the chocolate in the slow cooker.

4   Cover with the lid and cook on Low for 6–8 hours. Just before serving, remove the cinnamon stick and bay leaf, break the chocolate into pieces and stir into the dish until it has melted.

6. JUST YOU & ME?

S MART DISHES FOR YOU AND ME, or maybe just for me! A birthday, an anniversary, Valentine's Day, festivals and notable events – all are good excuses to push the boat out and take extra care to create a special slow-cooked meal for you and your partner. If you're dining solo, make a fuss of yourself to mark that special occasion. And, remember, your slow cooker is energy-saving compared to a meal for one or two taking hours in the oven.

Spend a little more money on fine ingredients, or go for size, like the whole salmon for the recipe on page 74, and splash the wine generously into the food when the recipe invites this. Then, topping up your glass and raising a toast, celebrate in style.

SEAFOOD IN A WINE & HERB SOUP

A luxury main meal soup, ideal for two but can easily be halved to serve one. Ask the fishmonger for small pieces of different fish.

SERVES 2	1 medium red onion
	2 garlic cloves
HIGH 1½–2½ hours	6 medium tomatoes
	Small bunch fennel
	Small bunch parsley
	1 small lemon
	300g/10½ oz mixed fish fillets, trout, bream or salmon
	Pinch of saffron threads

1 tbsp fish or vegetable bouillon powder
300ml/½ pint red wine
2 tbsp tomato purée
Freshly milled salt and black pepper
200g/7 oz mixed shelled shellfish, prawns, cockles or clams
1 tbsp capers
Hot crusty bread, to serve

1   Preheat the slow cooker on High while you prepare the ingredients.

2   Put the kettle on to boil. Finely chop the onion and crush the garlic. Roughly chop the tomatoes. Finely chop the herbs. Slice the lemon into 8 wedges. Cut the fish into bite-sized pieces.

3   Pour 150ml/¼ pint hot water into a jug and mix in the saffron threads, bouillon powder, wine, tomato purée and a little seasoning.

4   Put the onion, garlic and tomatoes evenly over the base of the slow cooker. Arrange the fish and shellfish on top. Scatter over the capers and half the chopped herbs. Pour over the wine mixture.

5   Cover with the lid and cook on High for 1½–2½ hours. Stir in the remaining chopped herbs just before serving in wide shallow bowls with hot crusty bread and lemon wedges.

SALMON & PRAWNS WITH VERMOUTH

A meal in a parcel. Salmon, prawns and vegetables with dill, lemon and vermouth flavourings cook in a paper and foil parcel with noodles cooking in the water alongside.

SERVES 2

HIGH 2–3 hours

4 spring onions
6 button mushrooms
2 small carrots
100g/3½ oz mange tout
½ small lemon
3 tbsp dry vermouth
1 tbsp balsamic vinegar

Freshly milled salt and black pepper
2 handfuls spinach leaves
300g/10½ oz salmon fillet, in one piece
4 prawns, with shells
Sprigs of dill
50g/5½ oz noodles

1   Preheat the slow cooker on High while you prepare the ingredients. Cut a large sheet of non-stick baking paper three times the size of the fish fillet. You also need extra thick foil.

2   Put the kettle on to boil. Thinly slice the spring onions and mushrooms. Coarsely grate the carrots and cut the mange tout into long, thin strips. Cut the lemon into 4 slices.

3   In a small bowl, mix the vermouth and balsamic vinegar with some seasoning.

4   Put the sheet of baking paper on a clean surface and pile the spinach leaves in the centre and top with the other vegetables. Lay the fish fillet across the vegetables and put the prawns on top.

5   Lift the paper up around the ingredients and scrunch to form a parcel, leaving space for the steam. Before you close the parcel, tuck the lemon slices and dill alongside the fish and pour over the vermouth mixture. Double wrap the parcel in foil.

6   Put the parcel into the slow cooker. Pour in sufficient hot water to come half-way up the sides of the pot. Cover with the lid and cook on High for 2–3 hours. Stir in the noodles, cover and cook for a further 15 minutes.

7   Lift the parcel from the cooker, carefully open to release the steam. With a slotted spoon remove and drain the noodles. Serve on hot plates.

Peppers with Spiced Cheese Stuffing

It may be necessary to trim the bases of the peppers to enable them to stand upright in the slow cooker – be careful you don't cut right through the flesh. Serve with a salad of crisp green leaves dressed with oil and vinegar.

SERVES 2
as a main dish,
4 as a starter

HIGH 2–4 hours

100g/3½ oz bulgur wheat
1 generous tsp vegetable bouillon powder
4 red or yellow peppers or a mixture
1 small red onion
Small handful of fresh parsley
100g/3½ oz feta cheese
100g/3½ oz mozzarella or Cheddar cheese

2 tbsp toasted pine kernels
½ tsp mixed spice
2 tbsp sultanas
2 tsp Dijon mustard
1 tbsp extra virgin olive oil
Salt and freshly milled black pepper

1   Preheat the slow cooker on High while you prepare the ingredients.

2   Put the kettle on to boil. Put the bulgur wheat into a bowl. Dissolve the bouillon powder in 200ml/7 fl oz boiling water (from the kettle). Stir half the stock into the wheat and leave to stand for 10 minutes until the liquid has been absorbed. Reserve the remaining stock.

3   Cut the tops off the peppers and reserve. Remove and discard the seeds and white membranes. Put the peppers and their tops into a large heatproof bowl and pour over sufficient boiling water (from the kettle) to cover them. Leave to stand for 5 minutes before draining.

4   Finely chop the onion and parsley. Cut the cheeses into small cubes.

5   Mix the bulgur wheat, onion, parsley and cheeses with the pine kernels, mixed spice, sultanas, mustard, oil and seasoning. Pile the mixture into the peppers, stand them in the slow cooker and top them with their lids. Pour the reserved stock around.

6   Cover with the lid and cook on High for 2–4 hours.

DUCK WITH POMEGRANATE JUICE

Pomegranate juice is readily available in cartons or bottles. It adds a rich, tart, slightly sweet flavour to this dish.

SERVES 2		
	1 medium red onion	2 tbsp cornflour
LOW 2–4 hours	4 spring onions	1 tbsp hoisin sauce
+ 15 minutes	2 large carrots	150ml/¼ pint pomegranate juice
	2 large courgettes	150ml/¼ pint chicken stock
	2 pak choi	Freshly milled black pepper
	2 duck breasts	150g/5½ oz noodles

1   Preheat the slow cooker on High while you prepare the ingredients.

2   Finely chop the onion. Cut the spring onions, carrots and courgettes into very thin strips. Finely shred the pak choi.

3   Heat a non-stick pan and cook the duck breasts until golden brown. Transfer the meat to a plate. Add the chopped red onion to the pan and cook for 5 minutes until beginning to brown. Stir in the cornflour, hoisin sauce, pomegranate juice, stock and a little seasoning. Heat until bubbling.

4   Arrange the vegetables over the base of the slow cooker. Put the duck breasts on top and pour over the onion and stock mixture.

5   Cover with the lid and cook on Low for 2–4 hours.

6   Whilst the dish is cooking, soak the noodles in water following the manufacturer's instructions. Drain the noodles, stir into the slow cooker, pushing them into the vegetables and liquid, cover and cook for a further 15 minutes.

LAMB CHOPS ON CARAMELISED SQUASH

The slow cooker is ideal when you want small quantities of food to cook ever so slowly in their own juices. Simply put all your ingredients (browning them first when necessary) into an ovenproof dish, covered with foil and surrounded by hot water, and let it simmer away gently until you are ready to eat.

SERVES 2	1 small acorn squash	4 lamb chops of your choice
	1 garlic clove	Salt and freshly milled black pepper
LOW 4–6 hours	1 tbsp olive oil	10 cherry tomatoes
	15g/½ oz butter	2 tbsp dry white wine
	1 tbsp soft light brown sugar	Lemon or lime wedges, to serve
	Pinch of chilli powder	

1   Preheat the slow cooker on High while you prepare the ingredients.

2   Put the kettle on to boil. Chop the squash and crush the garlic. Heat a large non-stick frying pan on the hob. When hot, add the oil and butter, swirling it round until melted. Add the squash and garlic, sprinkle with the sugar and chilli powder and brown quickly on both sides until the sugar has caramelised slightly. Transfer to an ovenproof dish that will fit comfortably inside the slow cooker.

3   Add the lamb chops to the hot pan and brown quickly on all sides. Lift them out and lay them on top of the squash. Season with salt and pepper, scatter the tomatoes over and sprinkle the wine on top.

4   Cover the dish securely with foil and stand it in the slow cooker. Pour round sufficient boiling water to come half-way up the sides of the dish.

5   Cover with the lid and cook on Low for 4–6 hours.

6   Carefully lift the dish out of the slow cooker and remove the foil. Spoon the lamb, tomatoes and squash onto warmed plates and serve with lemon or lime wedges for squeezing over.

LANCASHIRE LAMB SHANKS

This is loosely based on the traditional recipe for Lancashire Hotpot, and includes more or less the same ingredients. You could jazz it up by adding a squeeze of lemon juice and a handful of black olives just before serving.

SERVES 2	1 medium onion	15g/½ oz butter
	1 medium carrot	Few sprigs of fresh thyme
LOW 8–10 hours	500g/1 lb 2 oz potatoes	Salt and black pepper
	1 tbsp olive oil	300ml/½ pint lamb stock or vegetable stock
	2 lamb shanks	

1   Preheat the slow cooker on High while you prepare the ingredients.

2   Put the kettle on to boil. Chop the onion, thinly slice the carrot and cut the potatoes into small chunks.

3   Heat a large non-stick frying pan. When hot, add the oil and the lamb shanks and brown quickly on all sides. Lift out onto a plate.

4   Add the butter to the hot pan then toss in the onion, carrot and potatoes. Cook over medium heat for 8–10 minutes, stirring occasionally, until beginning to soften and brown.

5   Add the thyme, seasoning and stock to the pan. Bring just to the boil and transfer to the slow cooker.

6   Add the browned lamb shanks and their juices to the slow cooker, pushing them down snugly into the potatoes.

7   Cover with the lid and cook on Low for 8–10 hours until very tender.

Mustard Chicken with Whisky & Wild Mushrooms

Smothered in a whisky and marmalade sauce, the flavours of Scotland permeate succulent chicken joints. Use free-range chicken for lots more taste.

SERVES 2	1 large red onion	2 tbsp wholegrain mustard
	200g/7 oz mixed wild mushrooms	2 tbsp marmalade
LOW 4–6 hours	6 thyme sprigs	2 tbsp whisky
	2 tsp oil	300ml/½ pint chicken stock
	2 chicken quarters	Freshly milled salt and black pepper
	2 tbsp sesame seeds	2 tbsp double cream

1   Preheat the slow cooker on High while you prepare the ingredients.

2   Put the kettle on to boil. Finely chop the onion. If the mushrooms are large, tear into bite-sized pieces. Pull the leaves from the thyme sprigs.

3   Heat the oil in a pan and cook the chicken portions until golden brown on all sides. Transfer the chicken to the slow cooker. Add the onion to the pan and cook for 5 minutes until beginning to brown. Stir in the sesame seeds, mustard, marmalade, thyme leaves, whisky, stock and seasoning. Heat until almost bubbling.

4   Put the mushroom mixture into the slow cooker. Cover with the lid and cook on Low for 4–6 hours. Stir in the cream just before serving.

PHEASANT IN ORANGE & APPLE SAUCE

Choose a pheasant that will fit snugly into your slow cooker; alternatively, cut the bird into joints. Lovely with a salad of crisp chicory leaves, fresh orange segments and a few black olives.

SERVES 2	1 small onion
	1 small orange
LOW 4–6 hours	1 sharp eating apple
	200g/7 oz chestnut mushrooms
	1 tbsp olive oil
	15g/½ oz butter
	1 oven-ready pheasant, about 1.3kg/3 lb

25g/1 oz flour
300ml/½ pint chicken stock
150ml/¼ pint orange juice
150ml/¼ pint dry cider
Salt and freshly milled black pepper

1   Preheat the slow cooker on High while you prepare the ingredients.

2   Finely chop the onion. Finely chop the orange, skin and all, discarding any pips. Peel and quarter the apple, remove and discard its core, and cut into small pieces. Thickly slice the mushrooms.

3   Heat a large non-stick frying pan. When hot, add the oil and butter and brown the pheasant quickly all over. Transfer it to the slow cooker.

4   Add the onion, orange, apple and mushrooms to the hot pan and cook for 8–10 minutes, stirring occasionally, until beginning to soften and turn golden brown. Remove from the heat and stir in the flour. Gradually stir in the stock, orange juice and cider. Season with salt and pepper. Bring to the boil, stirring, and pour over the pheasant in the slow cooker.

5   Cover with the lid and cook on Low for 4–6 hours.

7. STRICTLY VEGETARIAN

VEGETABLES COME IN SUCH a myriad of types and varieties, and, if you take in beans and lentils, tofu and Quorn, the range of flavours and textures is unending. Everyone, vegetarians and carnivores alike, will love these exciting, enticing and strictly vegetarian recipes.

These recipes are ideal for mid-week entertaining because they are so varied and adaptable. Complete in themselves, many could easily be served (to more people) as an accompaniment. And here's an idea for any non-veggies tempted to look in this section – some meat or fish would go really well with several of these recipes.

Stimulating and satisfying as they are, these are dishes for every season.

FLAGEOLET & BLACK-EYED BEANS WITH PISTOU

Pistou is the French version of Italy's pesto, a mix of olive oil, basil and garlic.

SERVES 6–8	250g/9 oz flageolet beans	Pistou topping:
	250g/9 oz black-eyed beans	6 tomatoes
LOW 6–8 hours	2 medium red onions	2 garlic cloves
	2 celery sticks	A small bunch fresh basil
	2 green chillies (see page 14)	60g/2¼ oz shelled walnut pieces
	1 lime	3 tbsp olive oil
	1½ tbsp vegetable bouillon powder	Hot crusty bread, to serve
	Freshly milled black pepper	

1	Soak the beans overnight in plenty of cold water.

2	Preheat the slow cooker on High while you prepare the ingredients. Put the kettle on to boil. Finely chop the onions and thinly slice the celery sticks. Cut the chillies in half, remove and discard their seeds and stalks, and slice thinly. Finely grate the rind from the lime. Cut the lime in half and squeeze out the juice.

3	Drain the beans. Put into a large pan, cover with boiling water (from the kettle), bring back to the boil and cook rapidly for 10 minutes, then drain. Put the bouillon powder into a measuring jug and pour over 700ml/1¼ pints boiling water.

4	Put the beans into the slow cooker and add the prepared vegetables, chillies and lime rind and juice, then stir in the stock and season with pepper. Cover with the lid and cook on Low for 6–8 hours.

5	Whilst the dish cooks, prepare the topping. Put the tomatoes into a bowl, cover with boiling water (from the kettle) and leave for 1–2 minutes until the skins start to shrivel. With a slotted spoon lift out the tomatoes and leave to cool a little. With a sharp knife pull off the skins, cut in half, remove the cores and finely chop. Tip into a small dish, cover and chill until needed.

6	Finely chop the garlic, basil leaves and walnuts. Put them into a small dish, pour over the oil, season a little then cover and chill until needed.

7	Serve the bean mixture in wide bowls topped with a spoonful of tomato, a little pistou and lots of crusty bread.

ROOT VEGETABLES & RED BEANS
IN SPICED COCONUT SAUCE

The vegetables can be varied to suit your taste. Serve with freshly cooked rice or in shallow bowls with chunks of crusty bread. Any left over can be reheated the next day in the microwave or in a pan on the hob.

SERVES 6	2 medium onions	410g can red kidney beans
	2 garlic cloves	2 tbsp olive oil
LOW 6–8 hours	2.5cm/1 inch piece of ginger root	1 tsp cumin seeds
	2 medium leeks	500ml/18 fl oz vegetable stock
	2 medium carrots	1 generous tbsp curry paste
	2 medium parsnips	1 tsp ground turmeric
	500g/1 lb 2 oz celeriac	Salt and freshly milled black pepper
	200ml block of creamed coconut	Handful of fresh coriander leaves

1   Preheat the slow cooker on High while you prepare the ingredients.

2   Thinly slice the onions and finely chop the garlic cloves. Finely grate the root ginger. Cut the leeks, carrots, parsnips and celeriac into bite-size pieces. Cut the coconut into small pieces. Drain the beans.

3   Heat a large saucepan on the hob. When hot add the oil, onions, garlic, ginger and cumin seeds. Cook over medium heat for about 8 minutes or until beginning to soften and turn golden brown.

4   Add the leeks, carrots, parsnips and celeriac to the pan. Stir in the coconut, stock, curry paste, turmeric, seasoning and red beans. Bring just to the boil, stirring occasionally, and transfer to the slow cooker.

5   Cover with the lid and cook on Low for 6–8 hours.

6   Just before serving, roughly chop the coriander leaves and stir them in.

SPICED BEETROOTS & RED CABBAGE WITH TOFU

Beetroots are often overlooked as a hot vegetable, possibly because they colour the other ingredients. Here we've teamed them with other red or orange vegetables, given them a spicy taste and added tofu for extra protein.

SERVES 4–6

LOW 3–5 hours
+ 15–20 minutes

2 medium red onions
1 garlic clove
½ medium red cabbage
6 medium beetroots
1 small orange
300g/10½ oz firm tofu
300ml/½ pint vegetable stock
3 tbsp red wine vinegar

3 tbsp clear honey
2 tsp chilli sauce
2 tsp dried mixed herbs
¼ tsp ground cloves
Freshly milled salt and black pepper
Crème fraîche, to serve
Chopped fresh parsley, to serve

1   Preheat the slow cooker on High while you prepare the ingredients.

2   Finely chop the onions and crush the garlic. Cut the red cabbage in half, remove and discard the central core then thinly shred. Trim any stalks from the beetroots then remove the skin with a potato peeler. (Wear disposable gloves when handling beetroots to prevent your hands becoming discoloured.) Coarsely grate the beetroots. Finely grate the rind from the orange, cut in half and squeeze out the juice. Dice the tofu and chill until needed.

3   Pour the stock into a jug and stir in the vinegar, honey, chilli sauce, orange rind and juice, mixed herbs, cloves and a little seasoning.

4   Tip the vegetables into the slow cooker and pour over the stock mixture. Cover with the lid and cook on Low for 3–5 hours. Stir after the first 2 hours.

5   Stir in the tofu and cook for a further 15–20 minutes. Serve with a dollop of crème fraîche and sprinkle over a little parsley.

Vegetable Chilli with Pan-Fried Tofu

We sometimes like to fry tofu for a brown, crisp result, as in this recipe. You could, of course, leave the tofu as it is and stir it into the chilli for the final half to one hour of cooking. A suitable accompaniment might be rice, couscous or thick slices of crusty bread (plain or spread with garlic butter and toasted).

SERVES 6	1 large onion	Two 425g cans red kidney beans
	1 medium carrot	3 tbsp olive oil
LOW 5–7 hours	1 large celery stick	Two 400g cans chopped tomatoes
	1 garlic clove	450ml/¾ pint vegetable stock
	1 red pepper	2 tbsp tomato purée
	1 yellow pepper	Salt and freshly milled black pepper
	1–2 small red chillies (see page 14)	Two 250g packets marinated or smoked firm tofu

1   Preheat the slow cooker on High while you prepare the ingredients.

2   Finely chop the onion, carrot, celery and garlic. Halve the peppers, remove the seeds and stalks, and slice thickly. Finely chop the chillies. Drain the kidney beans.

3   Heat 1 tbsp oil in a large pan on the hob and add the onion, carrot, celery and garlic. Cook over medium heat for 8–10 minutes, stirring occasionally until beginning to soften and turn golden brown.

4   Stir in all the ingredients except the remaining oil and the tofu. Bring just to the boil and tip into the slow cooker.

5   Cover with the lid and cook on Low for 5–7 hours until the vegetables are very soft.

6   About 30 minutes before serving, drain the tofu and pat it dry with kitchen paper. Cut into bite-size cubes or strips. Heat the remaining 2 tbsp oil in a non-stick frying pan, add the tofu in batches, browning it quickly on all sides. Lift out and keep warm.

7   Serve the vegetable chilli topped with the browned tofu.

Aubergines, Potatoes & Carrots with Lemon Myrtle

Lemon myrtle is an Australian spice and adds a distinctive lemon flavour to dishes. Replace with lemon rind if you can't find it in the stores.

SERVES 4–6, or 6–8 as an accompaniment	1 red onion	500g carton passata
	500g/1 lb 2 oz carrots	1½ tbsp vegetable bouillon powder
	2 aubergines, weighing about 450g/1 lb	3 tsp ground lemon myrtle
	1 kg/2¼ lb small new potatoes	Freshly milled salt and black pepper
LOW 4–6 hours	Small bunch of fresh parsley	

1   Preheat the slow cooker on High while you prepare the ingredients.

2   Put the kettle on to boil. Finely chop the onion and carrots. Trim the stalks from the aubergines and chop into even-sized pieces. Leaving the skins on, cut each potato into quarters. Finely chop the parsley.

3   Tip the vegetables into the slow cooker and scatter over half of the parsley (save the remainder for later).

4   Add the passata, bouillon powder and lemon myrtle and pour over 700ml/1¼ pints boiling water.

5   Stir well, cover with the lid and cook on Low for 4–6 hours.

6   Stir in the remaining parsley and season if necessary.

Minestrone Stew

Though this is meant to be a main dish, it could also be served as a starter, with some crusty Italian-style bread such as ciabatta. To jazz it up, consider grilling cheese on thick slices of toast and serving them on top of the stew or, for meat eaters, you could stir in some crisp-fried bacon pieces or meaty sausages.

SERVES 6–8	2 large onions	3 tbsp olive oil
	2 garlic cloves	500g carton passata
LOW 8–10 hours	2 large carrots	1 litre/1¾ pints vegetable stock
	3 celery sticks	Salt and freshly milled black pepper
	2 leeks	¼ Savoy cabbage
	1 fennel bulb	Handful of fresh parsley
	410g can cannellini or haricot beans	Hard Parmesan-style cheese
	410g can chickpeas	Handful of small pasta shapes, such as shells

1   Preheat the slow cooker on High while you prepare the ingredients.

2   Finely chop the onions and garlic. Thickly slice the carrots, celery, leeks and fennel. Drain the beans and chickpeas.

3   Heat the oil in a large saucepan on the hob. Add the onions, garlic, carrots and celery and cook for about 10 minutes, stirring occasionally, until just beginning to soften and turn golden brown.

4   Add the leeks, fennel, beans, chickpeas, passata, stock and seasoning. Bring just to the boil and tip into the slow cooker.

5   Cover with the lid and cook on Low for 8–10 hours until the vegetables are tender.

6   Meanwhile, slice the cabbage very thinly and chop the parsley. With a potato peeler, shave off strips of the cheese.

7   About 30 minutes before serving, stir in the cabbage and pasta. Replace the lid and cook for a further 30 minutes until the pasta is soft.

8   Stir in the parsley and serve in bowls topped with cheese shavings.

Marrow with Bulgur Wheat, Pepper & Ginger Stuffing

A retro dish with an up-to-date filling.

SERVES 4	1 marrow	2 tbsp small raisins
		2 tbsp pine nuts
LOW 2–4 hours	Stuffing:	1 tbsp light soy sauce
	60g/2¼ oz bulgur wheat	2 tbsp chopped fresh herbs
	1 medium onion	Freshly milled salt and black pepper
	1 garlic clove	400g can chopped tomatoes
	1 medium red pepper	400ml/14 fl oz chicken or vegetable stock
	Small piece fresh root ginger	Chopped fresh parsley to serve

1 Preheat the slow cooker on High.

2 Put the kettle on to boil. Cut the marrow into thick slices, about 8cm/3¼ inches and scoop out the seeds. (Check they fit into the slow cooker in a single layer.) Tip the bulgur wheat into a bowl and pour in boiling water to cover. Chop the onion and crush the garlic. Cut the pepper in half, remove and discard the seeds and stalks, and finely chop. Grate the ginger root.

3 Drain the bulgur wheat in a sieve, pressing down with the back of a spoon to remove as much water as possible. Tip into a large bowl and stir in the rest of the stuffing ingredients, seasoning a little.

4 Spoon and press the stuffing into the marrow rings. Pour the tomatoes and stock into the slow cooker and stir to mix. With a fish slice carefully lift the marrow rings into the slow cooker (a little stuffing may escape but don't worry).

5 Cover with the lid and cook on Low for 2–4 hours. Carefully lift the marrow slices onto plates. Spoon over the sauce and sprinkle with parsley.

CREAMY SQUASH & SWEET POTATO CASSEROLE

This could just as easily be made entirely with sweet potatoes or with squash. It may not be the most attractive dish in the world but it tastes wonderful and we like the way the vegetables mash into the juices to give a chunky-yet-smooth texture. Serve it in shallow bowls with crusty bread for mopping up the creamy juices.

SERVES 4–6

LOW 2½–3½ hours
+ 30 minutes

1 red onion
800g/1¾ lb sweet potatoes
800g/1¾ lb squash, such as acorn or butternut
2 garlic cloves
2.5cm/1 inch piece of fresh ginger root
About 4 sun-dried tomatoes

1 tbsp vegetable bouillon powder
Freshly milled black pepper
2 medium courgettes
Small handful of mange touts
150ml/¼ pint double cream
Handful of fresh coriander leaves

1 Preheat the slow cooker on High while you prepare the ingredients.

2 Put the kettle on to boil. Finely chop the onion. Peel and cut the sweet potatoes into chunks. Peel and discard the seeds from the squash and cut the flesh into chunks. Finely chop or crush the garlic cloves. Finely grate the ginger root. Cut the sun-dried tomatoes into small strips.

3 Put the onion, sweet potatoes, squash, garlic, ginger root, bouillon powder, black pepper and tomatoes into the slow cooker and stir in 600ml/1 pint boiling water (from the kettle).

4 Cover with the lid and cook on Low for 2½–3½ hours until the vegetables are soft.

5 Meanwhile, thinly slice the courgettes and cut the mange touts into short lengths.

6 Gently stir the courgettes, mange touts and cream into the cooked vegetables, replace the lid and continue cooking for a further 30 minutes.

7 Just before serving, stir in the coriander leaves.

Lentils, Root Vegetables, Star Anise & Lemon

A robust, rustic dish which couldn't be simpler to prepare. Adapt the dish by using seasonal vegetables. Serve as a veggie meal with hot crusty garlic bread, with a sprinkling of grated cheese, or to accompany a curry dish or roast meats.

SERVES 6–8

LOW 6–8 hours

250g/9 oz lentils
2 large onions
2 large garlic cloves
3 medium parsnips
2 small turnips
1 large unwaxed lemon

1 tbsp dried mixed herbs
700ml/1¼ pints vegetable stock
10 peppercorns
2 star anise
1 bay leaf

1   Preheat the slow cooker on High while you prepare the ingredients.

2   Wash the lentils in plenty of cold water and drain. Finely chop the onions and crush the garlic. Peel, trim and chop the parsnips and turnips into even-sized smallish pieces. Cut the lemon into 6 wedges.

3   Put all the ingredients into the slow cooker. Cover with the lid and cook on Low for 6–8 hours. Stir twice after the first 2 hours. The lentils will soften and thicken the dish. Remove the bay leaf and star anise before serving.

QUORN CASSOULET

Hot garlic bread goes very well with this hearty meat-free dish.

SERVES 6		
	2 medium onions	2 tbsp black treacle
LOW 4–6 hours	1 medium carrot	Salt and freshly milled black pepper
+ 1 hour	2 celery sticks	Two 300g packets Quorn pieces, thawed if frozen
	2 garlic cloves	6 Quorn sausages, thawed if frozen
	Three 425g cans haricot beans	
	2 tbsp olive oil	Topping:
	450ml/16 fl oz vegetable stock	25g/1 oz butter
	2 tbsp tomato purée	6 tbsp fresh breadcrumbs
	2 tbsp wholegrain mustard	Small handful of chopped fresh parsley

1   Preheat the slow cooker on High while you prepare the ingredients. Thinly slice the onions, carrot and celery. Finely chop the garlic. Drain the beans.

2   Heat a large saucepan. When hot add the oil, onions, carrot and celery. Cook over medium heat for 8–10 minutes until beginning to soften and turn golden brown. Stir in the garlic and beans. Add the stock, tomato purée, mustard, treacle and seasoning. Bring just to the boil and transfer to the slow cooker.

3   Cover with the lid and cook on Low for 4–6 hours until the vegetables are very tender.

4   Meanwhile, heat the butter in a small non-stick pan and cook the breadcrumbs until crisp and golden. Stir in the parsley and leave to cool.

5   Stir in the Quorn pieces and sausages, replace the lid and continue cooking for 1 hour. Serve sprinkled with the topping.

8. PERFECT PASTA, RICE & GRAINS

HERE ARE SOME DISHES to prove how versatile your slow cooker can be – probably more so than you imagined. Most of these pasta, noodle and rice dishes cannot be left alone for hours and hours like the typical slow cooker dish; they are quicker to prepare, but will need your attention.

These recipes are great for the middle of the week, when time is at a premium, so put the slow cooker on straight away when you come home from work.

We've used an exciting selection of ingredients, including millet and barley which you might not have tried before.

PASTA, MUSHROOM & BEAN MEDLEY

This dish relies on ingredients tucked away in the store-cupboard and makes an ideal midweek supper that is quick to put together. Keep it veggie or make some last-minute additions: flaked canned tuna, torn pieces of roast chicken, chopped ham, or freshly cooked sausages hot from the grill or frying pan. Garlic bread goes well with it.

SERVES 4–6	1 red onion	2 tbsp soy sauce
	1 red or yellow pepper	1 tbsp vegetable bouillon powder
LOW 5–8 hours	285g jar mixed mushrooms in oil	2 tsp sugar
+ 30 minutes	265g can flageolet beans	250g/9 oz pasta twists
	400g can tomatoes	

1 Preheat the slow cooker on High while you prepare the ingredients.

2 Put the kettle on to boil. Finely chop the onion. Cut the pepper in half, remove and discard the seeds and stalk, and slice thinly. Drain the mushrooms and beans.

3 Put the onion, pepper, mushrooms and beans into the slow cooker and add the tomatoes, soy sauce, vegetable bouillon powder and sugar. Stir in 750ml/1¼ pints boiling water (from the kettle).

4 Cover with the lid and cook on Low for 5–8 hours.

5 Switch the slow cooker to High. Stir in the pasta twists, pushing them under the surface of the liquid. Replace the lid and continue cooking on High for about 30 minutes, stirring gently once or twice, or until the pasta is just soft.

TROUT & FENNEL PASTA

There's such a huge choice of pasta shapes; for a change, try coloured pasta, flavoured with beetroot, spinach, squid or herbs. Serve with salad leaves.

SERVES 4–6	4 spring onions	300g/10½ oz trout fillets
	1 green pepper	1 tbsp fish or vegetable bouillon powder
HIGH 2–3 hours	1 large fennel bulb	350g/12 oz green spinach-flavoured pasta or plain
	3 celery sticks	pasta spirals
	½ lemon	Freshly milled salt and pepper

1   Preheat the slow cooker on High while you prepare the ingredients.

2   Slice the spring onions. Halve the green pepper, remove the seeds and slice thinly. Finely chop the fennel and celery sticks. Grate the rind from the lemon and squeeze out the juice. Cut the trout into bite-size pieces.

3   Put the kettle on to boil. Put the bouillon powder into a jug and pour over 700ml/1¼ pints hot water.

4   Put the onions, pepper, fennel, celery, lemon rind and juice into the slow cooker. Pour over the stock.

5   Cover with the lid and cook on High for 2–3 hours. Then, 35–45 minutes before serving stir the pasta and trout into the slow cooker pushing it under the liquid, re-cover and cook until tender. Season if necessary before serving.

ORIENTAL CHICKEN WITH EGG NOODLES

A lovely light dish that couldn't be easier to make. The star anise and cinnamon stick subtly add their flavours to the sauce, which is allowed to soak into the egg noodles shortly before serving.

SERVES 4–6	8–12 skinned chicken thighs	1 star anise
	2.5cm/1 inch piece of fresh ginger root	1 cinnamon stick
LOW 3–5 hours	5 tbsp dry sherry	300ml/½ pint chicken stock
+ 10 minutes	3 tbsp brown sugar	250g packet of medium egg noodles
	5 tbsp soy sauce	A few spring onions, to serve

1   Preheat the slow cooker on High while you prepare the ingredients.

2   Trim the chicken thighs of any excess fat. Finely grate the ginger root.

3   Put 300ml/½ pint water into a saucepan on the hob and add the sherry, sugar, soy sauce, star anise, ginger root, cinnamon stick and stock. Bring just to the boil and transfer to the slow cooker.

4   Add the chicken thighs to the slow cooker, pushing them into the liquid.

5   Cover with the lid and cook on Low for 3–5 hours until the chicken is very tender.

6   Move the chicken to the sides of the slow cooker and add the noodles, pushing them gently under the surface of the liquid. Replace the lid and continue cooking for about 10 minutes, stirring and separating the noodles once or twice, until soft and ready to serve.

7   Finely chop some spring onions and scatter over the chicken and noodles to serve.

Mushroom & Parmesan Rice

Dried mushrooms are a useful store-cupboard stand-by and we like the added flavour they give to dishes. Use small pieces in this risotto and choose from oyster, portobello, morel and chanterelle, to name just a few. Or use 250g/9 oz fresh mushrooms.

SERVES 4–6	350g/12 oz easy-cook long grain rice	2 tsp olive oil
	1 red onion	½ tsp dried thyme
LOW 1–2 hours	1 garlic clove	70g/2½ oz dried mushrooms
	8 asparagus spears	Freshly milled salt and pepper
	70g/2½ oz Parmesan cheese	1½ tbsp vegetable bouillon powder
	50g/1¾ oz butter	

1 Preheat the slow cooker on High while you prepare the ingredients.

2 Put the kettle on to boil. Rinse the rice under running cold water and drain. Thinly slice the onion and crush the garlic. Cut the asparagus into short lengths. Grate the Parmesan cheese.

3 Heat the butter and oil in a medium pan and fry the onion for a few minutes until softened. Add the garlic and rice and cook, stirring, for 2 minutes. Stir in the thyme, mushrooms, asparagus and seasoning. Add the bouillon powder and pour over 1.2 litres/2 pints hot water.

4 Pour into the slow cooker. Cover with the lid and cook on Low for 1–2 hours, stirring gently after 1 hour. Before serving stir in the Parmesan cheese.

CHILLI BROWN RICE WITH PRAWNS & SEEDS

Brown rice is very nutritious and nutty. Sunflower and sesame seeds add crunch to this chilli prawn dish.

SERVES 4	1 medium red onion	Freshly milled salt and pepper
	350g/12 oz easy-cook long grain brown rice	200g/7 oz spinach leaves
LOW 3–4 hours	300ml/½ pint vegetable stock	250g/9 oz shelled prawns
	300ml/½ pint tomato juice	Small handful sunflower seeds
	1 tbsp chilli paste	Small handful pumpkin seeds
	1 tbsp Worcestershire sauce	

1   Preheat the slow cooker on High while you prepare the ingredients.

2   Finely chop the onion.

3   Put the onion and rice into the slow cooker and pour over the stock and tomato juice. Stir in the chilli paste, Worcestershire sauce and seasoning.

4   Cover with the lid and cook on Low for 3–4 hours. Then, 15–20 minutes before the end of the cooking time stir in the spinach leaves, prawns, sunflower and pumpkin seeds.

BROWN RICE WITH LEEKS, BACON & CHEESE

We like to use brown rice though you could, of course, use white instead (but make sure you use the easy-cook variety for best results). Serve it like risotto – as a starter or with a salad garnish as a main dish.

SERVES 4–6	250g/9 oz easy-cook brown rice	2 tbsp olive oil
	2 medium leeks	700ml/1¼ pints vegetable or chicken stock, or a
HIGH 1–1½ hours	1 garlic clove	mixture
	200g/7 oz button or chestnut mushrooms	About 125g/4½ oz mature Cheddar-style cheese
	About 200g/7 oz back bacon rashers	Chopped fresh parsley

1   Preheat the slow cooker on High while you prepare the ingredients.

2   Wash and drain the rice. Thinly slice the leeks and finely chop the garlic clove. Halve or thickly slice the mushrooms. With scissors, trim the rind from the bacon rashers and cut into small strips.

3   Heat a large non-stick frying pan on the hob. When hot add the oil and bacon. Cook over medium-high heat for about 5 minutes until just beginning to brown.

4   Add the leeks and garlic to the bacon and cook over medium heat for about 5 minutes, stirring occasionally, until the leeks have softened slightly but not browned.

5   Stir in the rice, then add the mushrooms and stock. Bring just to the boil and tip the mixture into the slow cooker, stirring gently.

6   Cover with the lid and cook on High for 1–1½ hours, stirring gently after 1 hour, until the rice is just soft and almost all the liquid has been absorbed.

7   Meanwhile, grate the cheese.

8   Serve topped with grated cheese and chopped parsley.

LAMB COUSCOUS

Couscous is made from the grain of semolina and used in North African cuisine. Serve with hot breads and mango chutney.

SERVES 4–6

LOW 2½–3½ hours

1 large red onion
2 garlic cloves
2 carrots
1 celery stick
1 courgette
100g/3½ oz okra
4 dried apricots
500g/1 lb 2 oz boneless lean lamb

2 tsp olive oil
½ tsp ground cumin
½ tsp ground ginger
2 tsp lamb bouillon powder
Freshly milled salt and pepper
350g/12 oz couscous
85g/3 oz pine nuts
1 tbsp fresh parsley

1   Preheat the slow cooker on High while you prepare the ingredients.

2   Finely chop the onion and garlic. Thinly slice the carrots, celery and courgette. Trim the okra. Quarter the apricots. Trim excess fat from the lamb and cut into bite-size pieces.

3   Put the kettle on to boil. Heat the oil in a large frying pan, add the lamb and cook for a few minutes until golden brown. Remove the lamb to a plate. Fry the onion and garlic until brown, stir in the carrots, celery, courgette, okra and apricots. Mix in the cumin, ginger, bouillon powder and seasoning and pour over 600ml/1 pint hot water. Heat until starting to bubble. Put into the slow cooker.

4   Cover with the lid and cook on Low for 2½–3½ hours. Meanwhile, tip the couscous into a large bowl and pour over cold water to cover. Then, 5–10 minutes before the end of the cooking time, drain the couscous and stir with the pine nuts and parsley into the slow cooker and replace the lid. Stir again before serving.

BARLEY PILAFF WITH LAMB & MUSHROOMS

Barley and lamb combine to make a dish that is richly flavoured and filling. Serve it with a crisp green salad.

SERVES 4–6	1 large onion	1 tbsp olive oil
	1 medium carrot	150ml/¼ pint dry white wine or vermouth
LOW 4–6 hours	1 garlic clove	500ml/18 fl oz lamb or vegetable stock
+ HIGH 1–1½ hours	150g/5½ oz chestnut mushrooms	Salt and freshly milled black pepper
	Small sprig of fresh rosemary	250g/9 oz pearl barley
	4–6 lamb leg steaks, each weighing about 175g/6 oz	

1   Preheat the slow cooker on High while you prepare the ingredients.

2   Finely chop the onion, carrot and garlic. Slice the mushrooms. Finely chop the rosemary leaves to make about 1 tsp. Cut each lamb steak into about 4 pieces.

3   Heat a large non-stick frying pan on the hob. When hot add the oil and the lamb in a single layer. Brown quickly on all sides and lift onto a plate.

4   Add the onion, carrot, garlic and mushrooms to the hot pan and cook over medium heat for about 5 minutes or until beginning to soften and turn golden brown.

5   Stir in the rosemary and wine or vermouth and bubble quickly for a few seconds. Add the stock and a little seasoning. Bring just to the boil and transfer to the slow cooker. Add the lamb and its juices, pushing it down into the liquid.

6   Cover with the lid and cook on Low for 4–6 hours until the lamb and vegetables are tender.

7   Switch the slow cooker to High and stir in the barley. Replace the lid and cook on High for a further 1–1½ hours or until the barley is tender.

Hot Cracked Wheat & Ham Salad

In place of ham, try adding thickly sliced smoked sausage. Any left-over salad can be served cold.

SERVES 4–6

HIGH 1 hour
+ 15 minutes

250g/9 oz bulgur wheat
1 medium onion
1 medium leek
1 tbsp olive oil
25g/1 oz butter
700ml/1¼ pints vegetable or chicken stock, or a
 mixture
2 tbsp Worcestershire sauce

2 tbsp tomato purée
1 tsp dried mint or a generous tbsp finely chopped
 fresh mint
4 small courgettes
4 tomatoes
Small handful of pine kernels
4–6 thick slices of cooked ham
Salt and freshly milled pepper

1   Put the bulgur wheat into the slow cooker and preheat it on High while you prepare the other ingredients.

2   Thinly slice the onion and leek.

3   Heat the oil and butter in a saucepan. Add the onion and leek and cook over medium heat for 5–10 minutes until softened and just beginning to turn golden brown.

4   Stir the stock into the onion mixture, together with the Worcestershire sauce, tomato purée and mint. Bring just to the boil and pour over the wheat in the slow cooker, stirring gently.

5   Cover with the lid and cook on High for 1 hour or until nearly all the liquid has been absorbed.

6   Meanwhile, finely chop the courgettes and tomatoes. Lightly toast the pine kernels in a dry frying pan until golden brown. Chop the ham.

7   Stir the courgettes, tomatoes and ham into the hot wheat, replace the lid and continue to cook for a further 15 minutes.

8   Season if necessary and serve topped with toasted pine kernels.

WARM MILLET SALAD

Millet is a cereal grass and often overlooked as an ingredient. Be careful not to overcook it. Delicious with other salad ingredients, or use as a filling for tortillas, pancakes or pitta bread.

SERVES 4–6	6 spring onions	1 tbsp lime juice
	1 garlic clove	1 tbsp vegetable bouillon powder
HIGH 1–2 hours	250g/9 oz millet seeds	Small handful broken walnut pieces
	2 tsp olive oil	Freshly milled salt and pepper
	1 tbsp mild curry paste	Large bag mixed small salad and herb leaves

1 Preheat the slow cooker on High while you prepare the ingredients.

2 Thinly slice the spring onions and garlic.

3 Heat a non-stick pan and when hot add the millet and 'toast' for a few seconds until golden and put to one side. (Watch it doesn't burn.)

4 Pour the oil into the pan, fry the spring onions and garlic for a few minutes until softened. Stir in the curry paste, lime juice, bouillon powder, walnuts and seasoning. Tip the millet back into the pan and pour over 700ml/1¼ pints hot water. Heat until boiling.

5 Pour into the slow cooker. Cover with the lid and cook on High for 1–2 hours. Stir in the salad leaves and serve immediately. (The leaves will wilt.)

9. HOT & SPICY, EASY PEASY!

THE SPICES OF THE WORLD can find their way into your slow cooker, and you can have a 'take-away' from your own kitchen on any day you choose and at any time you like. It's cheaper too, and the food can be guaranteed to be top quality, with ingredients sourced from your favourite supermarket, corner shop or specialist store.

Whether your fancy runs to Indian, Mexican, Chinese or Thai cuisine, you'll find something to entice and excite you on this global menu. Just add the appropriate sidelines to your 'take-away' – bread (nan or tortillas), poppadoms, pickles, chutneys and relishes – and the world is at your fingertips.

TARKA DHAL

A well-flavoured dish of creamy split peas and squash. For the 'tarka', onions and garlic are cooked in oil and tipped onto the dhal just before serving. It goes well with rice, nan bread or poppadums, chutneys, tomato and red onion salad, plain yogurt flavoured with freshly chopped mint, or with roast vegetables.

SERVES 6–8	250g/9 oz yellow split peas	1 tsp ground cumin
	500g/1 lb 2 oz piece of squash, such as butternut or	1 tsp tamarind paste
LOW 8–10 hours	acorn	Salt and freshly milled black pepper
	1 large onion	1 tbsp fresh lemon juice
	2 garlic cloves	
	2 red chillies (see page 14)	For the 'tarka':
	2 tomatoes	1 small onion
	1cm/½ inch piece fresh ginger root	2 garlic cloves
	2 tbsp oil	3 tbsp oil
	1 tsp ground coriander	

1   Soak the peas in plenty of cold water for several hours or overnight.

2   Preheat the slow cooker on High while you prepare the ingredients.

3   Drain the split peas. Remove and discard the peel and seeds from the squash and cut it into thin slices. Finely chop the onion, garlic and chillies. Chop the tomatoes and finely grate the root ginger.

4   Heat the oil in a large saucepan, add the onion, garlic and chillies and cook over medium heat for about 8 minutes, stirring occasionally, until slightly softened.

5   Add the coriander and cumin and cook, stirring, for 1 minute. Add the split peas, squash, tomatoes, ginger, tamarind paste, seasoning and 1 litre/1¾ pints water. Boil for 5–10 minutes and transfer to the slow cooker.

6   Cover with the lid and cook on Low for 8–10 hours until the peas are very soft. When stirred, the mixture should break up into a porridge-like consistency (for an extra smooth dhal, whizz the mixture with a hand-held stick blender). Adjust the seasoning to taste and stir in the lemon juice.

7   Meanwhile, thinly slice the onion for the tarka and finely chop the garlic. Just before serving, heat the oil in a frying pan and cook the onion and garlic over medium heat until soft and golden brown. Tip the tarka on top of the dhal to serve (take care because the mixture can spit ferociously as it hits the peas).

BIRYANI

A spicy fragrant feast-day meal cooked in one dish. Bags of frozen mixed shellfish work well here and, in place of individual spices, use a curry powder or paste. Serve with yogurt, pickles and nan bread to scoop up the rice mixture.

SERVES 6	1 large red onion	3 cardamom pods
	2 garlic cloves	1 tbsp lemon juice
LOW 4–6 hours	Small piece fresh root ginger	1 tbsp vegetable bouillon powder
	250g/9 oz basmati rice	350g/12 oz mixed shelled shellfish
	2 tbsp oil	3 tbsp sultanas
	½ tsp ground chilli powder	3 tbsp freshly chopped parsley
	½ tsp ground cumin	Freshly milled black pepper
	½ tsp ground coriander	Coriander leaves, to serve

1   Preheat the slow cooker on High while you prepare the ingredients.

2   Put the kettle on to boil. Finely slice the onion and garlic. Grate the ginger root. Wash the rice under running cold water and drain.

3   Heat the oil in a large frying pan, add the onion and garlic, cook for a few minutes until golden brown. Add the spices and rice and cook for 2 minutes, stirring continuously. Mix in the lemon juice, bouillon powder, pour over 400ml/14 fl oz water and bring just to the boil. Spoon into the slow cooker.

4   Cover with the lid and cook on Low for 4–6 hours. Then, 30 minutes before serving, stir in the shellfish, sultanas and parsley and re-cover. Season if necessary and serve topped with a few coriander leaves.

CHICKPEAS WITH CUMIN, GREEN CHILLIES & PARSLEY

The chickpeas are best soaked overnight before cooking, so start preparing the evening before. Though the rosemary is optional, it makes a lovely addition to the finished flavour. Serve with couscous or rice.

SERVES 6

LOW 8–10 hours

350g/12 oz dried chickpeas
1 large onion
2 garlic cloves
2 green chillies (see page 14)
2.5cm/1 inch piece fresh ginger root
2 tbsp olive oil
1 tbsp cumin seeds

1 tsp turmeric
1 sprig of fresh rosemary (optional)
150ml/¼ pint dry white wine or vermouth
400g can chopped tomatoes
700ml/1¼ pints vegetable stock
Salt and freshly milled black pepper
Handful of fresh flat-leaf parsley

1   Soak the chickpeas in plenty of cold water for at least 8 hours or overnight. Next day, drain them and put them into a large saucepan on the hob. Cover well with water and boil rapidly for 10 minutes.

2   Preheat the slow cooker on High while you prepare the rest of the ingredients.

3   Finely chop the onion, garlic and chillies. Finely grate the ginger root.

4   Heat the oil in a large pan on the hob and add the onion, garlic and cumin seeds. Cook over medium heat for 5–10 minutes, stirring occasionally, until lightly browned.

5   Stir in the chillies, ginger, turmeric and rosemary (if using) and cook for 1 minute. Add the wine or vermouth, bubble quickly for a few seconds, and then stir in the tomatoes, stock and a little seasoning. Drain the boiled chickpeas and stir them in. Bring the mixture just to the boil and transfer to the slow cooker.

6   Cover with the lid and cook on Low for 8–10 hours.

7   Before serving, adjust the seasoning to taste, roughly chop the parsley and stir it in.

THAI GREEN CHICKEN & VEGETABLE CURRY

Serve with fragrant rice.

SERVES 4–6		
	1 large onion	4–6 skinless, boneless chicken breasts
	1 carrot	2 tbsp oil
LOW 4–6 hours	2 celery sticks	1 tbsp Thai green curry paste
	1 red pepper	300ml/½ pint chicken or vegetable stock
	200g/7 oz green beans	2 tbsp light soy sauce
	1 garlic clove	200ml/7 fl oz coconut milk
	2.5cm/1 inch piece fresh ginger root	Handful of fresh coriander leaves
	1 lime	

1 Preheat the slow cooker on High while you prepare the ingredients.

2 Thinly slice the onion, carrot and celery. Halve the pepper, remove and discard the seeds and stalk, and chop roughly. Trim the beans and cut them into short lengths. Finely chop the garlic and finely grate the ginger root. Finely grate the rind from the lime and squeeze out its juice. Cut each chicken breast into about six pieces.

3 Heat the oil in a large non-stick pan and add the onion, carrot and celery. Cook over medium heat for 5–10 minutes, stirring occasionally, until softened and just beginning to brown.

4 Stir in the curry paste, garlic and ginger and cook for 1 minute.

5 Add the remaining ingredients, except for the coconut milk and coriander. Bring just to the boil and transfer to the slow cooker, pushing the ingredients down into the liquid.

6 Cover with the lid and cook on Low for 4–6 hours until the chicken and vegetables are tender. About 30 minutes before serving, stir in the coconut milk. Just before serving, stir in the coriander leaves.

CHILLI CHICKEN BOWL

This resembles the Chinese dish Chow Mein with a dash of chilli added. We have used dried chillies but you could, of course, use fresh (see page 14). Adjust the amount to suit your palate. The noodles are already cooked and just need stirring in before serving.

SERVES 4–6	1 onion	5 tbsp soy sauce, plus extra for serving
	2 carrots	1 tbsp sugar
LOW 4–6 hours	2 garlic cloves	Generous pinch of crushed chillies
+ 10–15 minutes	2.5cm/1 inch piece fresh ginger root	300g packet of fresh bean sprouts
	340g can sweetcorn	300g packet of straight-to-wok noodles
	225g can bamboo shoots	2 tsp sesame oil (optional)
	4–6 boneless, skinless chicken breasts	Toasted sesame seeds, to serve
	1 tbsp oil	

1   Preheat the slow cooker on High while you prepare the ingredients.

2   Finely chop the onion. Cut the carrots into short sticks. Finely chop the garlic. Finely grate the ginger root. Drain the sweetcorn and bamboo shoots. Cut each chicken breast into five or six pieces.

3   Heat the oil in a large frying pan on the hob. Add the onion, carrots, garlic and ginger root and cook over medium-high heat for 3–5 minutes, until just beginning to turn golden brown. Add the drained sweetcorn and bamboo shoots, the soy sauce, sugar and chillies, and 400ml/14 fl oz water. Bring just to the boil, stir in the chicken and transfer to the slow cooker.

4   Cover with the lid and cook on Low for 4–6 hours.

5   Gently stir in the bean sprouts, noodles and sesame oil (if using), replace the lid and continue cooking for 10–15 minutes.

6   Serve topped with toasted sesame seeds and hand round the soy sauce for sprinkling over.

CHICKEN DHAL

Dhal is usually served as an accompaniment to a curry. Here it takes centre stage. Serve with rice, pickles and hot nan bread.

SERVES 4–6	1 medium red onion	300ml/½ pint chicken stock
	1 garlic clove	300ml/½ pint coconut milk
LOW 3–5 hours	1 red chilli (see page 14)	1 tsp ground ginger
	4 skinned, boned chicken breasts	1 tsp ground cumin
	1 tbsp oil	1 tsp ground coriander
	200g/7 oz red lentils	6 cardamom pods

1   Preheat the slow cooker on High while you prepare the ingredients.

2   Finely chop the onion and garlic. Cut the chilli in half, remove and discard the seeds and stalks, and slice thinly. Cut the chicken into strips.

3   Heat the oil in a frying pan, add the onion and cook over medium heat for a few minutes until just beginning to soften. Stir in the garlic. Increase the heat, add the chicken and cook, stirring occasionally, until golden brown.

4   Put the chicken mixture into the slow cooker and stir in the remaining ingredients.

5   Cover with the lid and cook on Low for 3–5 hours.

Spiced Lamb with Apricots

Succulent lamb flavoured with curry powder and cumin. Serve with couscous or rice.

SERVES 6

LOW 6–8 hours

2 medium onions
2 garlic cloves
1 red pepper
150g/5½ oz dried apricots
2 tbsp plain flour
2 tbsp curry powder
1 tsp ground cumin

1 tsp ground turmeric
½ tsp salt
1kg/2¼ lb lean lamb cubes
2 tbsp oil
400g can chopped tomatoes
1 generous tsp vegetable bouillon powder
2 tbsp lemon juice

1   Preheat the slow cooker on High while you prepare the ingredients.

2   Finely chop the onions and garlic. Halve the pepper, remove and discard the seeds and stalk, and chop roughly. Halve the dried apricots.

3   Mix together the flour, curry powder, cumin, turmeric and salt and toss the lamb cubes in the mixture (easy to do in a large plastic food bag).

4   Heat the oil in a large non-stick frying pan. Quickly brown the lamb in batches and transfer to the slow cooker.

5   Add the onions and garlic to the hot pan and cook over medium heat for about 8 minutes, stirring occasionally, until just beginning to soften and brown. Add the red pepper, apricots, tomatoes, bouillon powder and 300ml/½ pint water. Bring just to the boil and stir the mixture into the lamb in the slow cooker, pushing the apricots under the surface.

6   Cover with the lid and cook on Low for 6–8 hours until the lamb and vegetables are very tender. Stir in the lemon juice just before serving.

Chilli Beef & Chorizo

Quick and easy to prepare. Serve with hot crusty garlic bread, jacket potatoes or spaghetti, and extra chilli sauce for those who prefer it hotter.

SERVES 4	1 large onion	200g/7 oz sweetcorn
	2 garlic cloves	400g can chopped tomatoes
HIGH 3–5 hours	150g/5½ oz spicy sausage, such as chorizo	1 tsp chilli sauce
	or kabanas	2 tsp beef bouillon powder
	250ml/9 oz lean minced beef	Freshly milled salt and black pepper
	400g can chickpeas	Natural yogurt, to serve

1   Preheat the slow cooker on High while you prepare the ingredients.

2   Finely chop the onion and crush the garlic. Thinly slice the sausage.

3   Heat a non-stick pan, and, when hot, tip in the sausage and beef and cook for about 5 minutes until lightly brown, stirring and breaking up the meat with a wooden spoon. With a slotted spoon remove the meat and put onto a plate. Add the onion and garlic to the pan and cook for 5 minutes until softened. Return the meat to the pan and stir in the chickpeas, sweetcorn, tomatoes, chilli sauce, and bouillon powder. Pour over 300ml/½ pint hot water and heat until starting to bubble. Tip into the slow cooker.

4   Cover with the lid and cook on High for 3–5 hours. Season if necessary and serve with a little yogurt spooned on top.

CHINESE PORK WITH CASHEWS

Serve with rice and pickled ginger root.

SERVES 4–6	6 spring onions	1 tbsp olive oil
	Small piece of root ginger	150ml/¼ pint chicken stock
LOW 3–5 hours	1 red pepper	1 tbsp clear honey
	1 red chilli (see page 14)	1 tbsp tamarind paste
	200g/7 oz mange tout	Large handful bean sprouts
	350g/12 oz lean boneless pork	12 cashew nuts
	1 tbsp cornflour	

1   Preheat the slow cooker on High while you prepare the ingredients.

2   Thinly slice the spring onions. Peel or scrape the ginger root and finely grate. Cut the pepper and chilli in half, remove and discard their seeds and stalks, and slice thinly. Cut the mange tout diagonally into strips. Cut the pork into thin slices and dust with the cornflour.

3   Heat the oil in a frying pan, add the spring onions and cook over medium heat for a few minutes, stirring occasionally, until just beginning to soften. Stir in the ginger, red pepper and chilli. Increase the heat, add the pork and cook, stirring occasionally, until golden brown.

4   Put the pork mixture into the slow cooker, stir in the stock, honey and tamarind paste. Heat until just bubbling. Pour into the slow cooker.

5   Cover with the lid and cook on Low for 3–5 hours. Then, 30 minutes before serving stir in the mange tout and bean sprouts, cashew nuts and re-cover.

MILD LAMB CURRY WITH COCONUT

Equally good made with chicken in place of lamb. Serve with rice, mango chutney and pickles.

SERVES 4	500g/1 lb 2 oz boneless, lean lamb	½ tsp ground cloves
	1 tbsp olive oil	½ tsp ground cinnamon
LOW 3–5 hours	400g chopped tomatoes	300ml/½ pint coconut milk
	¼ tsp turmeric	150ml/¼ pint vegetable stock
	¼ tsp cayenne pepper	150ml/¼ pint crème fraîche

1   Preheat the slow cooker on High while you prepare the ingredients.

2   Cut the lamb into bite-size pieces.

3   Heat the oil in a frying pan, add the lamb and cook until golden brown. Stir in the remaining ingredients except the crème fraîche and heat until starting to bubble.

4   Pour into the slow cooker. Cover with the lid and cook on Low for 3–5 hours. 10 minutes before serving stir in the crème fraîche.

10. LEISURELY PUDS

THERE'S A SPECIAL APPEAL about puddings – they are so comforting and mouthwatering that they make you want to settle down and relax in order to savour them to the full. We love old-fashioned puddings, though we've given some of our recipes an up-to-date twist; there's plenty of fruit, and lots of sweetness and stickiness. If you have a sweet tooth then just get stuck in; if you're health-conscious you can still find something here with just a hint of indulgence.

On weekdays or on special occasions these puddings are equally delicious, and they go well throughout the year too, summer and winter alike.

Some of these dishes are cooked straight in the slow cooker. For others the mixture is put into a dish which is then placed inside the slow cooker, surrounded by hot water. This technique is used for Sticky Butterscotch Pudding (page 152) and Egg Custard with Lime & Maple Syrup (page 157).

PECAN-FILLED APPLES

Check that the apples will fit inside your slow cooker. For a change replace the apples with firm pear halves.

SERVES 4

HIGH 2–4 hours

4 small Bramley cooking apples
90g/3¼ oz pecan nuts
2 tbsp clear honey
1 tsp ground ginger

25g/1 oz butter
150ml/¼ pint unsweetened apple juice

1   Preheat the slow cooker on High while you prepare the ingredients.

2   With a sharp knife score around the fattest part of the apples and remove the cores. Finely chop the pecan nuts.

3   In a bowl, mix together the nuts, honey and ginger. Spoon the mix into the apples, pressing it down well and top each with a little butter.

4   Arrange the apples in the slow cooker and pour over the apple juice.

5   Cover with the lid and cook on High for 2–4 hours.

Brioche, Banana & Cranberry Pudding

Odd but true: jam, sultana and custard sandwiches on top of banana and cranberries. Warming, comforting and very very tempting. We used fresh cranberries, but frozen are available all year round. Ring the changes with other seasonal fruits.

SERVES 4–6

HIGH 2–3 hours

40g/1½ oz butter, plus extra for greasing
1 orange
4 large bananas
140g/5 oz cranberries
3 tbsp soft brown sugar
8 thick slices sweetened bread (brioche)

2 tbsp apricot jam
500g carton custard
Handful sultanas
2 medium eggs
400ml/14 fl oz milk
Extra custard, to serve

1   Preheat the slow cooker on High while you prepare the ingredients.

2   Lightly grease the inside of the slow cooker pot. Finely grate the rind from the orange, cut the orange in half and squeeze out the juice. Thinly slice the bananas.

3   Put the cranberries and banana slices into the slow cooker, sprinkle over the sugar and pour over the orange juice. Lightly butter a slice of bread, spread with some apricot jam and a little custard and scatter over a few sultanas. Cover with a slice of bread to make a 'sandwich' and cut in half. Repeat with the remaining bread slices.

4   Arrange the sandwiches evenly over the top of the fruit. Beat the eggs into the milk and pour over the pudding.

5   Put the dish into the slow cooker. Pour in sufficient hot water to come half-way up the sides of the dish. Cover with the lid and cook on High for 2–3 hours. Serve with extra custard.

PLUMS & BERRY CRUMBLE

Fruit crumble is an age-old pudding which never seems to be out of fashion. The rubbed-in crumble topping mix freezes really well without setting into a solid mass. Spoon onto prepared fruits and cook.

SERVES 4–6	600g/1 lb 5 oz red plums	90g/3¼ oz soft brown sugar
	140g/5 oz plain wholemeal flour	300g/10½ oz raspberries and blackberries or
HIGH 2–4 hours	40g/1¾ oz rolled oats	blueberries
	½ tsp ground cinnamon	
	90g/3¼ oz butter	

1   Preheat the slow cooker on High while you prepare the ingredients.

2   Halve and stone the plums.

3   Mix the flour, oats and cinnamon in a large bowl. Cut the butter into small cubes and add to the flour mixture. Using your fingertips, rub in the butter until the mixture resembles fine crumbs (or do this part in a food processor). Stir in 40g/1½ oz of the sugar.

4   Arrange the plums, raspberries and blackberries over the base of the slow cooker pot. Sprinkle over the remaining sugar and 6 tbsp cold water. Cover with the crumble mixture, but don't press it down too firmly.

5   Cover with the lid and cook on High for 2–4 hours.

CHOCOLATE GINGER PUDDING

Serve this sticky pudding with a generous spoonful of thick yogurt, crème fraîche or custard; or our favourite – a scoop of vanilla ice cream.

SERVES 4–6	100g/3½ oz soft butter, plus extra for greasing	150g/3½ oz self-raising flour
	2 medium eggs	25g/1 oz cocoa powder
HIGH 3–4½ hours	4 large pieces of stem ginger in syrup	
	100g/3½ oz soft brown sugar	

1   Preheat the slow cooker on High while you make the pudding.

2   Put the kettle on to boil. Butter the inside of a 1.2 litre/2 pint pudding bowl. Lightly beat the eggs. Drain the ginger and chop into small pieces.

3   Beat the butter with the sugar until light and fluffy. Gradually beat in the eggs. Sift the flour and cocoa powder over the top and, with a large metal spoon, fold in gently, adding the chopped ginger and 1–2 tbsp of the syrup from the jar.

4   Spoon the mixture into the prepared bowl. Cover with a sheet of non-stick baking paper and then a sheet of foil. Scrunch up the edges, pressing them onto the sides of the bowl to make a secure seal.

5   Stand the bowl in the slow cooker and pour in sufficient boiling water (from the kettle) to come half-way up the sides of the bowl.

6   Cover with the lid and cook on High for 3–4½ hours until gently firm to the touch and cooked through.

7   Carefully lift the bowl from the slow cooker. Turn the pudding out onto a warmed plate for serving.

TROPICAL FRUIT PUDDING

This pudding is served straight from the slow cooker. Putting a sheet of non-stick paper under the lid helps prevent condensation from dripping onto the sponge as it cooks. Accompany it with pouring cream, yogurt, ice cream or hot custard.

SERVES 6–8	125g/4½ oz soft butter, plus extra for greasing	125g/4½ oz soft light brown sugar
	1 small pineapple	2 medium eggs
HIGH 2½–3½ hours	1 ripe mango	Few drops of vanilla extract
	2 large bananas	150g/5½ oz self-raising flour
	2 passion fruit	25g/1 oz desiccated coconut

1   Rub the inside of the slow cooker with a little butter then preheat on High while you prepare the ingredients.

2   Prepare the pineapple by cutting off the top and base, and removing and discarding the skin, including the 'eyes'. Cut the trimmed fruit into quarters lengthways and remove and discard the hard core. Cut the remaining fruit into small chunks. Peel the mango, slice the flesh from the stone and chop roughly. Peel and thickly slice the bananas.

3   Put the pineapple, mango and banana in an even layer in the slow cooker. Halve the passion fruit and, using a teaspoon, scrape the seeds and juice over the top.

4   Put the butter, sugar, eggs and vanilla extract into a large mixing bowl and sift the flour over the top. Beat well for 2–3 minutes until light and smooth, and then fold in the coconut.

5   Spoon the mixture evenly over the fruit in the slow cooker (no need to level the surface).

6   Place a large sheet of non-stick paper over the top and secure it down with the lid.

7   Cook on High for 2½–3½ hours until the sponge is firm to the touch.

SQUASH & RAISIN PUDDING

The squash gives its sweetness to this pudding and helps to keep it moist. Carrot would work just as well. Serve warm with thick cream, yogurt or custard, or a quick fruit sauce made by blending a can of apricots in light syrup.

SERVES 6–8	3 tbsp pine kernels	150g/5½ oz self-raising flour
	150g/5½ oz soft butter, plus extra for greasing	½ tsp baking powder
HIGH 2½–3½ hours	150g/5½ oz squash, such as butternut, weighed after peeling and discarding seeds	1 tsp ground mixed spice
	3 medium eggs	3 tbsp sultanas or raisins
	150g/5½ oz soft light brown sugar	3 tbsp milk

1   Preheat the slow cooker on High while you prepare the ingredients.

2   Put the kettle on to boil. In a small non-stick frying pan, lightly toast the pine kernels until golden brown and leave to cool. Butter the inside of a 17.5–20cm/7–8 inch ovenproof soufflé dish or deep cake tin and line its base with a circle of non-stick baking paper. Grate the squash. Lightly beat the eggs.

3   Beat the butter with the sugar until light and fluffy. Gradually beat in the eggs. Sift the flour, baking powder and mixed spice over the top and, with a large metal spoon, fold in. Lightly fold in the grated squash, sultanas or raisins, toasted pine kernels and milk.

4   Spoon the mixture into the prepared dish. Cover with a sheet of non-stick baking paper and then a sheet of foil. Scrunch up the edges, pressing them onto the sides of the dish to make a secure seal.

5   Stand the dish in the slow cooker and pour in sufficient boiling water (from the kettle) to come half-way up its sides.

6   Cover with the lid and cook on High for 2½–3½ hours until firm to the touch and cooked through.

CHOCOLATE & RUM FONDUE

This is sheer indulgence and chocoholics' idea of heaven! Give your guests long-handled forks for spearing marshmallows and the like for dipping into the molten chocolate. We like to use a chocolate with at least 50 per cent cocoa solids. Sometimes, we replace the rum with brandy or orange liqueur. This mixture also makes a luxurious sauce to serve with fruit or ice cream.

SERVES 4–6

LOW 1 hour
+ 30 minutes

200g/7 oz dark chocolate
150ml/¼ pint double cream
3 tbsp golden syrup
3 tbsp rum

To serve – choose a selection:
Marshmallows
Cubes of crusty bread

Cubes of cake, such as Madeira or sweet brioche
Sponge fingers
Crisp biscuits or cookies
Nuts, such as Brazils, walnuts or pecan halves
Fresh fruit, such as orange segments, chunks of fresh
    pineapple, banana
Dried fruit, such as apricots or dates

1   Preheat the slow cooker on High while you prepare the ingredients.

2   Put the kettle on to boil. Break the chocolate into a heatproof bowl and add the cream and golden syrup. Cover securely with foil.

3   Put the bowl into the slow cooker and pour round sufficient boiling water (from the kettle) to come half-way up its sides.

4   Cover with the lid and cook on Low for 1 hour.

5   Stir well and replace the foil securely. Replace the lid and continue cooking for a further 30 minutes.

6   Just before serving, stir in the rum.

7   Serve with your chosen selection of 'dippers'.

STICKY BUTTERSCOTCH PUDDING

Custard is our favourite accompaniment for this rather sophisticated pudding. Best results come if the dates are soaked and cooled before adding them to the pudding mixture.

SERVES 6–8		
HIGH 3½–4½ hours	**Topping:** 25g/1 oz butter, plus extra for greasing 50g/1¾ oz soft brown sugar 5 tbsp double cream **Pudding:** 175g/6 oz pitted dates	1 tea bag, such as Earl Grey 2 medium eggs 85g/3 oz soft butter 115g/4 oz soft brown sugar Few drops of vanilla extract 150g/5 oz self-raising flour

1. Chop the dates and put them into a small bowl with the tea bag. Pour over 120ml/4 fl oz boiling water (from the kettle). Cover and leave to cool.

2. Preheat the slow cooker on High while you prepare the rest of the ingredients.

3. Put the kettle on to boil. Butter a deep 15–18cm/6–7 inch ovenproof dish (such as a soufflé dish) and line the base with a circle of non-stick paper. Lightly beat the eggs.

4. To make the topping, melt the butter and stir in the sugar and cream. Spread the mixture over the paper in the dish.

5. To make the pudding, beat the butter with the sugar until light and fluffy. Gradually beat in the eggs and vanilla extract. Sift the flour over the top and, with a large metal spoon, fold in lightly.

6. Remove the tea bag from the dates, squeezing it to release any liquid. Stir the dates and their juices into the pudding mixture. Spoon it into the dish (no need to level the surface).

7. Cover with a sheet of non-stick paper and then a sheet of foil. Scrunch the edges tightly to the sides of the dish, securing them well.

8. Stand the dish in the slow cooker and pour round sufficient boiling water (from the kettle) to come half-way up its sides.

9. Cover with the lid and cook on High for 3½–4½ hours until firm to the touch and cooked through.

10. Run a knife round the side of the dish and turn the pudding out onto a warmed plate. Remove the paper and serve.

Plum Pudding

This pudding, with its dumpling topping, is suitable for all sorts of fruit – try rhubarb, apples, raspberries or cherries. The amount of sugar depends on the sweetness of the fruit. To make a smaller pudding, halve the quantities and assemble it in a suitable sized ovenproof dish. Cover securely with non-stick paper and foil, and put into the slow cooker with boiling water to come half-way up its sides.

SERVES 8

**LOW 3–5 hours
+ HIGH 45 minutes**

1kg/2¼ lb plums
8 tbsp elderflower cordial
4 tbsp caster sugar, plus extra if necessary

Topping:
200g/7 oz self-raising flour

1 tsp baking powder
50g/1¾ oz butter
2 tbsp caster sugar
1 medium egg
100ml/3½ fl oz milk
2 tbsp demerara sugar

1   Preheat the slow cooker while you prepare the fruit.

2   Halve the plums and remove and discard their stones. Put the fruit into the slow cooker and stir in the cordial and 2 tbsp water. Sprinkle with the sugar.

3   Cover with the lid and cook on Low for 3–5 hours until very soft.

4   To make the topping, sift the flour with the baking powder. Using fingertips, rub in the butter until the mixture resembles fine breadcrumbs. Stir in the sugar. Lightly beat the egg with the milk and stir into the flour mixture to make a soft dough.

5   Taste the plum mixture and adjust the sweetness if necessary.

6   Drop eight spoonfuls of the dough on top of the hot fruit (do not spread them out).

7   Cover with the lid and cook on High for 45 minutes until the topping is firm to the touch and cooked through.

8   Leave to stand, uncovered, for 5 minutes before sprinkling with the demerara sugar and serving.

CHOCOLATE RICE PUDDING

Delicious hot, by itself or with poached fruits, or cold, topped with yogurt or cream.

SERVES 4–6

HIGH 4–6 hours

Butter, for greasing
140g/5 oz pudding rice
3 tbsp cocoa powder
150ml/¼ pint coconut milk
1 litre/1¾ pints milk

90g/3¼ oz raisins
60g/2¼ oz sugar
½ tsp vanilla extract
60g/2¼ oz semi-sweet chocolate
Toasted flaked almonds, to serve

1   Put the kettle on to boil. Grease the inside of the slow cooker. Rinse the rice in cold water.

2   Put the cocoa into a small bowl and stir in 3 tbsp hot water. Mix until smooth and stir in 3 tbsp cold water.

3   Put all of the pudding ingredients, except the chocolate and the almonds, into the slow cooker.

4   Cover with the lid and cook on High for 4–6 hours, stirring once or twice during the final 2 hours. Stir in the chocolate until melted and serve scattered with almonds.

EGG CUSTARD WITH LIME & MAPLE SYRUP

All the flavour of crème caramel but without the hassle of making the caramel.

SERVES 6

HIGH 2–3 hours

Butter, for greasing
½ lime
2 tbsp maple syrup
100g/3½ oz caster sugar
400ml/14 fl oz full fat milk

150ml/¼ pint single cream
5 medium egg yolks
Extra maple syrup, for serving

1   Preheat the slow cooker on High while you prepare the ingredients. Lightly grease and line the base of a deep 18cm/7 inch ovenproof dish with non-stick baking paper. (Check the dish fits inside your slow cooker.)

2   Put the kettle on to boil. Finely grate the lime rind. Swirl the maple syrup over the base of the buttered dish.

3   Pour the sugar, milk and cream into a heavy-based pan and stir in the lime rind. Stirring with a wooden spoon bring almost to the boil (don't let it boil) and remove from the heat.

4   Tip the egg yolks into a bowl and lightly beat. Pour over the hot milk mixture and pour through a fine sieve into the dish. Cover securely with foil.

5   Put the dish into the slow cooker. Pour in sufficient hot water to come half-way up the sides of the dish.

6   Cover with the lid and cook on High for 2–3 hours until firm. Remove from the slow cooker, leave until cold and chill overnight. Loosen the edges and turn onto a plate. Serve cold with extra maple syrup.

GREENGAGES WITH COCONUT

A coconut and Madeira-crumb meringue tops delicious greengages.

SERVES 4–6

HIGH 2–4 hours

600g/1 lb 5 oz greengages
400g/14 oz Madeira cake
90g/3¼ oz desiccated coconut
3 medium egg whites

100g/3½ oz soft brown sugar
¼ tsp ground nutmeg over top

1   Preheat the slow cooker on High while you prepare the ingredients.

2   Halve and stone the greengages. Finely crumble the Madeira cake.

3   Mix the cake crumbs and coconut in a bowl. In another clean bowl stiffly whisk the egg whites. Slowly whisk in the sugar until it forms soft peaks. Carefully fold into the coconut mix.

4   Arrange the greengages in the base of the slow cooker pot. Pour over 6 tbsp cold water. Cover with the coconut mixture, swirl the surface and sprinkle over the nutmeg.

5   Cover with the lid and cook on High for 2–4 hours until the fruit is tender.

11. Cool Cakes

CAKES FROM THE SLOW COOKER? Can this be for real? Well yes, but these are not exactly the most familiar types of cake. In fact, their flavours and textures are most unusual. These cakes are all moist and sticky; with a dollop of cream or syrup, or some fruit on the side. Most would make excellent puddings.

There's something sophisticated and luxurious about these cakes. They will also be irresistible – some of them will be eaten so rapidly they won't have a chance to go cold. So this is serious temptation. Don't put up any resistance, you're bound to give in.

Extra Chocolaty Chocolate Cake

A treat for all chocolate lovers! For the best flavour use chocolate that contains at least 50 per cent cocoa solids (we like to use 70 per cent). It goes well alongside a cup of strong coffee or as a dessert with thin cream poured over.

SERVES 6

HIGH 1½–2½ hours + 15 minutes

40g/1½ oz dark chocolate
125g/4½ oz soft butter
125g/4½ oz caster sugar
25g/1 oz ground almonds
2 medium eggs
3 tbsp milk
100g/3½ oz self-raising flour

½ tsp baking powder
25g/1 oz cocoa powder

Icing:
50g/1¾ oz dark chocolate
25g/1 oz butter
1 tbsp double cream

1   Preheat the slow cooker while you prepare the ingredients and make the cake.

2   Put the kettle on to boil. Butter the inside of an 18–20cm/7–8 inch ovenproof soufflé dish or deep cake tin. Line the base with a circle of non-stick baking paper.

3   Chop the chocolate into small pieces. Put the butter, caster sugar, almonds, eggs and milk into a large mixing bowl. Sift over the flour, baking powder and cocoa. Beat well for 2–3 minutes until smooth, light and fluffy. Fold in the chocolate pieces.

4   Spoon the mixture into the prepared dish or tin, roughly levelling the surface.

5   Put the dish into the slow cooker and pour round sufficient boiling water (from the kettle) to come half-way up its sides.

6   Cover with the lid and cook on High for 1½–2½ hours until firm to the touch and cooked through.

7   Meanwhile, prepare the icing ingredients. Break the chocolate into a small ovenproof bowl and add the butter and cream. Cover securely with clear film or foil.

8   Carefully lift the cake out of the slow cooker and put the bowl of icing ingredients in its place. Replace the lid and cook for about 15 minutes or until the chocolate has melted.

9   Leave the cake to stand in its dish for 5 minutes before running a knife around the sides if necessary to loosen them, then turning the cake out onto a wire rack lined with a sheet of non-stick baking paper (to prevent the cake sticking to the rack). Leave to cool.

10 As soon as the chocolate has melted, stir the icing ingredients until smooth and glossy. Spread the mixture over the top of the cake and leave to cool completely.

Chocolate Cake with a Nut Topping

Nutty, cocoa and cinnamon cake topped with a squidgy topping.

SERVES 6	100g/3½ oz butter, plus extra for greasing	¼ tsp ground cinnamon
	60g/2¼ oz shelled, blanched nuts, such as almonds, pecan or hazelnuts	2 tbsp cocoa powder
HIGH 3–4 hours		200g/7 oz light brown caster sugar
	3 medium eggs	Icing sugar, to dust
	100g/3½ oz self-raising flour	Melted chocolate, to pour

1   Preheat the slow cooker on High while you prepare the ingredients.

2   Lightly grease and line the base of a deep 18cm/7 inch cake tin with non-stick baking paper. (Check the tin fits inside your slow cooker.) Put the kettle on to boil. Roughly chop the nuts. Take one of the eggs and separate the yolk from the white.

3   Sift the flour, cinnamon and half of the cocoa powder into a large bowl. Add the 2 remaining eggs plus the extra yolk, half the sugar and half the chopped nuts. Beat until well mixed and fluffy. In a clean bowl whisk the egg white until stiff, fold in the remaining sugar and whisk until soft. Stir in the remaining cocoa powder and nuts.

4   Spoon the cake mixture into the prepared tin and swirl the meringue mixture on top.

5   Put the tin into the slow cooker. Pour in sufficient hot water to come half-way up the sides of the tin. Cover with the lid and cook on High for 3–4 hours.

6   Lift the tin out of the slow cooker and leave to stand for 15 minutes. Loosen the edges with a knife and carefully turn out. (It doesn't matter if the surface breaks.) Leave to cool, dust thickly with icing sugar and cut into wedges. Serve with a little melted chocolate poured or drizzled over the top.

CARDAMOM & GINGER CAKE WITH SESAME & PINE NUTS

You might be more familiar with the use of cardamom in savoury dishes, but it adds a lovely flavour to cakes and biscuits as well. Here we've teamed it with the peppery sweet flavour of ginger and added sesame seeds and pine nuts for crunch.

SERVES 8

HIGH 3–4 hours

100g/3½ oz butter, plus extra for greasing
100g/3½ oz wholemeal self-raising flour
½ tsp baking powder
½ tsp ground cardamom
1 tsp ground ginger
100g/3½ oz light brown caster sugar

2 medium eggs
1 tsp vanilla extract
1 tbsp clear honey
60g/2¼ oz sesame seeds
2 tbsp pine nuts
Icing sugar, to dust

1 Preheat the slow cooker on High while you prepare the ingredients.

2 Lightly grease and line the base of a deep 18cm/7 inch cake tin with non-stick baking paper. (Check the tin fits inside your slow cooker.) Put the kettle on to boil.

3 Sift the flour, baking powder, cardamom and ginger into a large bowl. Cut the butter into small cubes and add to the flour mixture. Using your fingertips, rub the butter into the flour and spices until the mixture resembles fine crumbs (or do this part in a food processor). Add the sugar, eggs, vanilla, honey and sesame seeds. Beat until well mixed, soft and smooth.

4 Spoon into the prepared tin, smooth the surface and scatter the pine nuts over the top.

5 Put the tin into the slow cooker. Pour in sufficient hot water to come half-way up the sides of the tin. Cover with the lid and cook on High for 3–4 hours.

6 Lift the tin out of the slow cooker and leave to stand for 5 minutes. Loosen the edges with a knife and turn out. Leave to cool, dust with icing sugar and cut into wedges.

Sticky Pineapple & Cinnamon Cake

Good just as it is, with a cup of tea or coffee, or cut into wedges and served with a generous spoonful of crème fraîche for dessert.

SERVES 6	125g/4½ oz butter, plus extra for greasing	1½ tsp ground cinnamon
	125g/4½ oz crystallised pineapple	175g/6 oz golden syrup
HIGH 1½–2½ hours	2 medium eggs	125g/4½ oz soft light brown sugar
	125g/4½ oz self-raising flour	Icing sugar

1 Preheat the slow cooker while you prepare the ingredients and make the cake.

2 Put the kettle on to boil. Butter the inside of an 18–20cm/7–8 inch ovenproof soufflé dish or deep cake tin. Line the base with a circle of non-stick baking paper.

3 Chop the pineapple into small pieces. Lightly beat the eggs. Sift the flour with the cinnamon. With the fingertips, rub the butter into the flour until the mixture resembles fine breadcrumbs (alternatively you could do this in a food processor). Add the golden syrup, sugar and eggs and beat until smooth. Stir in the pineapple.

4 Spoon the mixture into the prepared dish or tin, roughly levelling the surface.

5 Put the dish into the slow cooker and pour round sufficient boiling water (from the kettle) to come half-way up its sides.

6 Cover with the lid and cook on High for 1½–2½ hours until firm to the touch and cooked through.

7 Carefully lift the dish out of the slow cooker and leave the cake to stand for 5 minutes. Run a knife around the sides to loosen them, then turn the cake out onto a wire rack lined with a sheet of non-stick baking paper (to prevent the cake sticking to the rack). Leave to cool completely.

8 Just before serving, sift a little icing sugar over the top.

Lemon Drizzle Polenta Cake

You'll find this cake irresistible.

SERVES 6	125g/4½ oz soft butter, plus extra for greasing	125g/4½ oz polenta (cornmeal)
	2 medium eggs	125g/4½ oz icing sugar
HIGH 2½–3 hours	2 lemons	
	100g/3½ oz caster sugar	
	100g/3½ oz self-raising flour	

1   Preheat the slow cooker while you prepare the ingredients and make the cake.

2   Put the kettle on to boil. Butter the inside of an 18–20cm/7–8 inch ovenproof soufflé dish or deep cake tin. Line the base with a circle of non-stick baking paper.

3   Lightly beat the eggs. Finely grate the rind from one lemon and squeeze the juice from two (you will need about 7 tbsp lemon juice).

4   Beat the butter with the sugar until light and fluffy. Gradually beat in the eggs. Sift the flour over the top and add the polenta and 4 tbsp lemon juice. Using a large metal spoon, fold in, until the mixture is smooth.

5   Spoon the mixture into the prepared dish or tin, roughly levelling the surface. Put the dish into the slow cooker and pour round sufficient boiling water (from the kettle) to come half-way up its sides.

6   Cover with the lid and cook on High for 2½–3 hours until firm to the touch and cooked through.

7   Meanwhile, make the drizzle mixture by blending the remaining 3 tbsp lemon juice with the icing sugar until smooth.

8   Carefully lift the dish out of the slow cooker and leave the cake to stand for 5 minutes. Run a knife around the sides to loosen them, then turn the cake out onto a wire rack lined with a sheet of non-stick baking paper (to prevent the cake sticking to the rack). Using a fine skewer, make several holes in the top of the warm cake and slowly spoon the drizzle over the top. Leave to cool before serving.

Sticky Oat, Orange & Walnut Cake

Lovely – a sticky, nutty, orange-flavoured cake made with oats for flavour and texture.

SERVES 6–8

HIGH 3–4 hours

100g/3½ oz butter, plus extra for greasing
1 small orange
60g/2¼ oz walnut pieces
60g/2¼ oz golden syrup

60g/2¼ oz light brown sugar
100g/3½ oz rolled oats
60g/2¼ oz self-raising flour
2 medium eggs

1   Preheat the slow cooker on High while you prepare the ingredients.

2   Lightly grease and line the base of a deep 18cm/7 inch ovenproof dish with non-stick baking paper. (Check the dish fits inside your slow cooker.) Put the kettle on to boil. Finely grate the rind from half the orange. Cut the orange in half and squeeze out the juice. Roughly chop the walnuts.

3   Put the butter, syrup and sugar into a small pan. Gently heat, stirring continuously until melted. Remove from the heat and pour into a large bowl. Stir in the oats, flour, orange rind and juice, then add the eggs (the mixture mustn't be too hot). Mix thoroughly and spoon into the prepared dish.

4   Cover the dish tightly with foil and put into the slow cooker. Pour in sufficient hot water to come half-way up the sides of the dish. Cover with the lid and cook on High for 3–4 hours.

5   Lift the dish out of the slow cooker and leave to stand for 5 minutes. Loosen the edges with a knife and turn out. Leave to cool and cut into wedges.

12.

TOP PRESERVES

You ALWAYS NEED PRESERVES at the ready. We don't know where we would be without our home-made supply of preserves, and a great way to make these is to use your slow cooker.

Curds, butters, conserves, relishes, chutneys and sauces – all of them can be created in a slow cooker. They will then be at hand to serve (as spreads, fillings, toppings or accompaniments) with toast, pancakes or ice cream, with cheeses and with cold meats, or in a host of other ways. And just think of all those recipes containing instructions to spread, drizzle or spoon preserves onto the mixture for cooking or onto the finished dish.

Preserves can be stored quite happily in the fridge. They won't be there long, though, because they are so useful and so appetising you will soon need to make some more.

DATE & APRICOT RELISH

A sticky sweet relish which can be spooned onto pancakes or ice cream or served with cold ham or smoked mackerel. Store in the refrigerator and use within three months.

MAKES ABOUT 1.3kg/3 lb	1 unwaxed lemon	250g/9 oz granulated sugar
	350g/12 oz dried pitted dates	400ml/14 fl oz unsweetened apple juice
	350g/12 oz dried apricots	25g/1 oz butter
LOW 4–6 hours	2 green apples	1 tsp ground allspice

1   Preheat the slow cooker on High while you prepare the ingredients.

2   Finely grate the rind from the lemon, cut in half and squeeze the juice. Finely chop the dates and apricots. Cut the apples into quarters, remove the cores and cut the fruit into small pieces (no need to peel them).

3   Put all the ingredients into the slow cooker and stir well.

4   Cover with the lid and cook on Low for 4–6 hours, stirring occasionally after the first 2 hours until cooked and thickened.

5   Stir well before spooning into warm sterilised jars and sealing.

Autumn Fruit Spread

Though this preserve is cooked over two days, it requires only a little attention from the cook and is ideal for using up windfalls. The skins are left on the fruit to give the best possible flavour to the finished fruit butter. Spread it on hot toast or use it to sandwich cakes or meringues. Store in the refrigerator and use within 4 weeks.

MAKES ABOUT 900g/2 lb

LOW 8–10 hours + HIGH 5–8 hours

1kg/2¼ lb cooking apples
1kg/2¼ lb firm pears
1 lemon
225g/8 oz golden caster sugar

½ tsp ground cinnamon
250ml/9 fl oz apple juice

1   Cut the apples and pears into quarters, remove their stalks and cores (leave their skins in place) and chop into small pieces. Finely grate the rind from the lemon and squeeze out its juice.

2   Toss the chopped fruit with the lemon rind and juice, sugar and cinnamon. Tip the mixture into the slow cooker, pressing it down gently to make an even layer. Pour the apple juice over the top.

3   Cover with the lid and cook on Low for 8–10 hours or overnight until the fruit is very soft.

4   Mash and stir the fruit well.

5   Switch the slow cooker to High and continue cooking, uncovered, for a further 5–8 hours or until the mixture is very thick.

6   Press the mixture through a sieve and discard the skins. Spoon the fruit purée into warmed, sterilised jars and seal.

APPLE, PLUM & WALNUT CHUTNEY

The long, gentle cooking creates wonderfully mature flavours in this chutney. You will want to start eating it as soon as it has cooled – try it with cheeses and cold meats or spooned into a bacon sandwich. It is best kept in the refrigerator and used within 2 months.

MAKES ABOUT 1.25kg/2¾ lb

HIGH 5–8 hours

675g/1½ lb cooking apples
250g/9 oz firm red plums
2 medium onions
2 garlic cloves
1 small red chilli (see page 14)

200g/7 oz walnut pieces
150ml/¼ pint red or white wine vinegar
450g/1 lb soft light brown sugar
1 tsp mixed spice
1 tsp ground ginger

1   Preheat the slow cooker on High while you prepare the ingredients.

2   Cut the apples into quarters and remove their cores and chop (no need to peel them). Halve the plums, remove their stones and chop. Finely chop the onions and garlic. Remove the stalk and seed from the chilli, and slice thinly. Roughly chop the walnuts.

3   Put all the ingredients into the slow cooker and mix well before levelling the surface.

4   Cover with the lid and cook on High for 5–8 hours, stirring occasionally, until very soft and thick.

5   Spoon into warmed, sterilised jars and seal.

Red Pepper Chutney

It won't be as sweet but try this recipe with green, orange or yellow peppers. Keep refrigerated and use within 6–8 weeks.

MAKES ABOUT 1.6kg/3½ lb

LOW 4–6 hours

1 kg/2¼ lb red peppers
2 red chillies (see page 14)
3 green apples
2 medium red onions
2 garlic cloves
200g/7 oz sultanas

300ml/½ pint vinegar, cider or red wine
225g/8 oz soft brown sugar
2 tsp fennel seeds
1 tsp ground cloves
1 tsp salt
1 tsp ground black pepper

1   Preheat the slow cooker on High while you prepare the ingredients.

2   Cut the peppers and chillies in half, remove and discard the seeds and stalks, and finely chop. Cut the apples into quarters, remove the cores and cut the fruit into small pieces (no need to peel them). Finely chop the onions and the garlic.

3   Tip the chopped fruits and vegetables into the slow cooker and stir in the remaining ingredients.

4   Cover with the lid and cook on Low for 4–6 hours, stirring twice, until thick.

5   Stir well before spooning into warm sterilised jars and sealing.

CITRUS CURD

There is nothing to beat the citrusy tang of home-made curd. It makes a lovely filling for cakes or meringues, as well as for spreading on fresh bread or hot toast. Use unwaxed fruits if possible. The curd should be stored in the refrigerator and used within 4 weeks – that's if you can resist it!

MAKES ABOUT 1kg/2¼ lb	2 large lemons	450g/1 lb caster sugar
	1 lime	4 medium eggs
	1 small orange	
LOW 3–4 hours	125g/4½ oz unsalted butter	

1   Scrub and dry the fruit. Finely grate the rind from the lemons, lime and orange, and squeeze out their juice. Cut the butter into small pieces.

2   Put the citrus rinds and juice into a pan on the hob and add the butter and sugar. Heat gently, stirring, until the butter has melted and the sugar has dissolved. Leave to cool.

3   Meanwhile, preheat the slow cooker on High. Put the kettle on to boil.

4   Beat the eggs and stir them into the cooled mixture. Strain into a 1.2 litre/2 pint pudding bowl (straining removes any stringy pieces of egg white).

5   Cover with a sheet of non-stick paper and then a sheet of foil. Scrunch the edges tightly to the sides of the dish, securing them well.

6   Stand the dish in the slow cooker and pour round sufficient boiling water (from the kettle) to come half-way up its sides.

7   Cover with the lid and cook on Low for 3–4 hours, stirring once or twice after the first 1½ hours if possible, until the curd has thickened.

8   Pour into warmed, sterilised jars and seal.

CHILLI CHOCOLATE SAUCE

Rich, dark, spicy Mexican sauces are used to add a smooth, rich flavour to meat and poultry dishes. The combination of chocolate and chilli may be a surprise but they do complement each other. Be bold: try a little with plain sorbet. Keep in the refrigerator and use within 2–3 weeks.

MAKES ABOUT 1.25kg/2¾ lb

HIGH 2½–3 hours + 30 minutes

500g/1 lb 2 oz piece of squash or pumpkin
200g/7 oz dried apricots
Small piece of fresh root ginger
3 red chillies (see page 14)

225g/8 oz plain dark chocolate
500ml/18 fl oz unsweetened apple juice
140g/5 oz sesame seeds

1   Preheat the slow cooker on High while you prepare the ingredients.

2   With a spoon, scoop out the seeds from the squash or pumpkin. Cut away the thick peel and chop the flesh into even-sized pieces. Quarter the apricots. With a small, sharp knife scrape the skin from the root ginger and finely grate. Cut the chillies in half, remove and discard the seeds and stalks, and finely chop. Coarsely grate the chocolate and reserve until later.

3   Tip the squash or pumpkin into the slow cooker and add the apricots, ginger and chillies. Pour over the apple juice and stir well.

4   Cover with the lid and cook on High for 2½–3 hours stirring once.

5   Stir in the sesame seeds, re-cover and cook for a further 30 minutes.

6   Remove the lid and use a stick blender to whizz the sauce smooth.

7   Scatter over the grated chocolate and stir until melted. The sauce should be quite thick.

8   Stir well before spooning into warm sterilised jars and sealing.

13.   CLEVER EXTRAS

THERE'S MANY A MEAL that can be enhanced by the addition of some well-judged, last-minute extras. Extras can provide added textures, crunch or bite, or fresh, contrasting flavours and colour to complement the pleasures of the principal dish. And you might, of course, want to make a dish go further; if so, pastry, scones or garlic bread add substance to your main meal and can set it off a treat.

There are good things here to stir in, like the pesto or curry paste, or to sprinkle over, like the crushed crisps, nachos or tortillas, or to fold in, like the rice noodles, or to serve alongside, like the stir-fried or steamed vegetables.

All these clever extras can give a final flourish to a meal as it makes its way to the table. Last-minute additions can freshen up a dish by adding crunch, a complementary flavour or a pastry, bread or scone topping. All are added towards, or at, the end of the cooking time. We've given both sweet and savoury suggestions.

Pastry

Ready-made pastry makes it easy to transform dishes into pies. Lift the cooked dish in its pottery liner out of the slow cooker and top with a sheet of short-crust or flaky pastry or buttered sheets of filo pastry and bake in a hot oven until risen and golden. Or pre-cook discs or shapes of pastry and put a couple on top of each serving.

Scones

In place of pastry, try sweet or savoury scones. Use a basic recipe and flavour with chopped fresh herbs, such as rosemary, parsley or oregano, cheese and mustard or nuts, lemon rind, ground ginger or cinnamon.

Parcels

Fish or shellfish can be wrapped in a foil parcel and put on top of vegetables cooking in the slow cooker.

Concentrated Sauces

Add extra flavour with a spoonful or two of red or green pesto, horseradish cream, mint jelly, cranberry sauce or tapenade.

Noodles

Rice noodles only need soaking in cold water; drained and added towards the end of the cooking time, they give a complete meal in one pot.

CRUNCHY THINGS

Plain or flavoured crisps, nachos, tortilla chips, biscuits, meringues, brandy snaps or ice cream cornets can be lightly crushed and scattered over the dish.

BREADS

Toasted breads made from thinly sliced bagels, sweet brioche, wedges of flour tortillas, mini nan breads flavoured with garlic, tomato or cheese make a tasty topping to bean, meat, fish or fruit dishes.

DROP IN SOME DUMPLINGS

Add dumplings to your favourite stews during the final stages of cooking. Simply sift 100g/3½ oz self-raising flour with 1 tsp baking powder and a little seasoning, and stir in 50g/1¾ oz shredded suet. Mix in sufficient cold water to make a soft dough and drop balls of the mixture on top of the stew, cover and continue cooking for 30–40 minutes.

ROASTED AND TOASTED

Oven-roasted or pan-fried fruits and vegetables such as onion rings, pepper slices, apple wedges and orange slices add another dimension. Toasted breadcrumbs, nuts and coconut all give added crunch.

ADDED BITE

Stir-fried or steamed vegetables will add colour and 'bite'.

FRESH HERBS

Adding fresh herbs just before serving will intensify the flavours.

GREMOLATA AND SALSAS

A spoonful of finely chopped fresh herbs, garlic and lemon rind adds extra zest. Or include tomatoes, chilli and a little oil for a real zing.

FINISH WITH A SWIRL

Flavour single or double cream, natural yogurt, crème fraîche or smooth tofu with fresh herbs, spices, finely chopped nuts, grated citrus rind, fruit purées, syrups or a little alcohol.

MAYONNAISE

Stir crushed garlic, tomato purée, wholegrain mustard or chopped fresh herbs into mayonnaise. Add a small amount to finished dishes.

SIFTED THINGS

For a speedy decoration, sift icing sugar, cocoa powder and drinking chocolate over desserts. Demerara sugar adds crunch and can be browned under a hot grill.

PRALINE

Delicious with desserts, praline is sugar dissolved in water and boiled until golden and then set hard. You could use crushed peanut brittle.

INDEX